SIXTEENTH–CENTURY POLYPHONY

LONDON : GEOFFREY CUMBERLEGE
OXFORD UNIVERSITY PRESS

SIXTEENTH – CENTURY POLYPHONY

A Basis for the Study of Counterpoint

By

ARTHUR TILLMAN MERRITT

PROFESSOR OF MUSIC, HARVARD UNIVERSITY

CAMBRIDGE, MASSACHUSETTS
HARVARD UNIVERSITY PRESS
1954

DISTRIBUTED IN GREAT BRITAIN BY
GEOFFREY CUMBERLEGE
OXFORD UNIVERSITY PRESS
LONDON

PRINTED AT THE HARVARD UNIVERSITY PRINTING OFFICE
CAMBRIDGE, MASSACHUSETTS, U. S. A.

ACKNOWLEDGMENTS

A special debt of gratitude is due to my students of counterpoint who have worked so enthusiastically every year on this branch of technical study. Without their wholehearted cooperation I should not have presumed to offer the present book. Grateful acknowledgment must be made to Dr. Archibald T. Davison for his unfailing encouragement and countless valuable suggestions.

A. T. M.

CAMBRIDGE, MASSACHUSETTS
June, 1939

CONTENTS

INTRODUCTION

IN recent years two books [1] have appeared in English which have stimulated the study of counterpoint and inspired teachers and students to make of it something more than the tonal mathematics it has succeeded in becoming in the last two hundred years. These books are invaluable because they have cut the Gordian knot which prevented so many theorists and teachers in that period from studying counterpoint as music. They are not textbooks, but they have done much because they advocate basing the study of counterpoint on actual music, and they have shown how far theory has strayed from practice in the course of time. Dr. Knud Jeppesen has since published a textbook [2] in which he has incorporated his ideas from the earlier book into a discipline. His analysis of the style of Palestrina is admirable, and I have profited immeasurably from it, but even he retains the old method in the early stages of the study.

It is a great shame that such an indispensable branch of musical study as counterpoint should have fallen on such evil days, shutting itself up in a technical vacuum completely removed from music. Music, like all the arts, changes in form and expression as time goes on — its whole history illustrates this — and it *must* change to express the feelings of each new generation. But this does not mean that, for the sake of gaining a technique, one must devitalize the study of its elementary stages as elementary counterpoint has so long been devitalized.

Historically, in the period which preceded the introduction

---

[1] R. O. Morris, *Contrapuntal Technique in the Sixteenth Century* (Oxford: The Clarendon Press, 1922) and Knud Jeppesen, *The Style of Palestrina and the Dissonance* (London: Oxford University Press, 1927).

[2] *Kontrapunkt* (Leipzig: Breitkopf & Härtel, 1935); English translation, *Counterpoint* (New York: Prentice-Hall, 1939), by Dr. Glen Haydon.

of the monodic style and the thorough bass — that is, roughly up to the end of the sixteenth century — counterpoint was the basis of practically all musical composition. After the coming of opera more emphasis was placed on the harmonic aspect of music, because composers found that harmony is more suitable for dramatic expression than counterpoint; in fact, it may be said that the dramatic style and real counterpoint are not often to be reconciled. On the other hand, seventeenth-century composers continued to write contrapuntally practically every type of music except the dramatic: witness, for example, the non-dramatic compositions of Frescobaldi, Schütz, and Purcell.

With the firm establishment of the major-minor mode about the end of the seventeenth century, harmony as we commonly understand it managed to wrest the palm from counterpoint and to assume the more important role. Although it is true that Bach and Handel have never had any superiors in the ability to weave lines together to create a beautiful contrapuntal fabric, they did this ordinarily on a harmonic basis within the frame of the major-minor mode. Their compositions have a harmonic flow which actually compels the individual lines to comply with it. The fact that the lines seem to comply so readily and yet have such individuality serves to impress us all the more with the tremendous skill of these composers; they do not appear to be restrained in the slightest by the fact that they weave their lines over progressions that are basically harmonic. Some — not many — later composers, like Mozart, Mendelssohn, and Brahms, followed more or less in their footsteps, employing counterpoint as they saw fit, always, however, increasing their harmonic vocabulary.

In the nineteenth century generally, counterpoint practically fell out of sight in much of the music for the pianoforte. The piano is at its best when used as a percussive instrument or in the manner of a harp, and at its worst when used to play music with a contrapuntal texture. And since it was by all odds the

prima donna among instruments throughout the nineteenth
century, it is not hard to understand why there was not more
interest in counterpoint at the time. It is a wonder there was so
much, and the greatest wonder of all is that counterpoint as a
study should ever have continued. It did degenerate, naturally
enough, into what most people considered a dry and academic
study — a kind of necessary evil. It was not considered useless
by most thoughtful students, for they saw that by means of it,
distasteful as it was, they could more quickly acquire the ability
to juggle notes. But there was hardly any artistic end in view.
One took a *cantus firmus* and put other voices through the hoop
around it, being careful only not to fall into any traps or disobey
any rules. The rules for this game were supposedly deduced
from the compositions of the sixteenth century, the so-called
Golden Age of counterpoint. But throughout the early and
middle romantic period people generally knew little about the
Golden Age, and cared less. The rules of counterpoint were
(and unfortunately are still for the most part) second-, third-,
or fourth-hand, being originally derived from a textbook of
counterpoint by Fux.[3] Fux's method was a synthesis of former
methods, and consisted of a careful and logical arrangement of
the whole study of counterpoint into the five "species" or five
consecutive steps which were to be followed. He knew and
analyzed Palestrina and his contemporaries, but he saw and
heard them through his own eighteenth-century eyes and ears —
which were harmonic eyes and ears. His perception was keen,
however, and his method was good at the time; it was sys-
tematic, and although his book was arbitrary, as most elementary
textbooks have to be, he constantly drew attention in it to actual
music and cited examples from musical literature. It was not
positively non- or antimusical, as some of its imitators have
become.

    Counterpoint textbooks have never ceased to appear, and,

[3] J. J. Fux, *Gradus ad Parnassum* (Vienna, 1725).

like all imitations, they have generally grown more and more diluted and arbitrary, until many modern ones are ridiculous. They almost invariably retain the five species laid down by Fux two hundred years ago, but each text varies the rules of the game according to the caprice of its author. The basis of the exercises is always harmonic, some authors being so conservative as to allow only one harmony per measure. The object of the procedure is — if one may flatter it by using the verb — to animate the harmony by means of notes of certain values, but one must go to the bitter end of the exercise without changing those values. Only in the fifth, or last, species — the so-called florid species — is there any permission to vary the rhythm; it never occurs to the author that rhythmic variety is the very soul of good contrapuntal music. Moreover, the exercises in these books are never more than ten to sixteen measures long. No problems of musical construction are involved in such short bits, and all the student has to do is to juggle notes until he gets to the end — a feat not easy to perform, it is true, if he obeys all the rules, for the handicaps are as great as the author chooses to make them. Another peculiar inconsistency in this old method is that, while *canti firmi* are used and certain sixteenth-century rules or practices have persisted, the whole system is based on the eighteenth-century major-minor mode. The result is a composite of styles: modal rules and regulations combined with major tonality, and the whole administered in single phrases a few measures long. It is impossible to relate the product to any great music that has ever existed, and, let us hope, to any that will ever exist in the future.

The purpose of the present book is to get away from such unmusical procedure and to base the study of counterpoint on actual contrapuntal music. There is no reason why any technique should become so rarefied as to lose all relation to the ultimate aim for which its study is intended. The modern student of composition needs technical training no less than the student of past times; in fact, it may fairly be said that he needs contrapuntal training even more than the nineteenth-century student, because modern composition is very often contrapuntal in texture. On the other hand, the student of musical history, or for that matter the musical amateur, is also in need of technical training in counterpoint, both because of the contrapuntal character of much modern music and because of the increased interest nowadays in the music of the older contrapuntal periods. There is no reason why at least the early study of the subject should be different for these different kinds of students. It is a great mistake to believe that one must be a musical genius in order to study music technically, and that one is on the road to becoming a composer if one has studied harmony and counterpoint. There are comparatively few persons in the world who have enough gift to become successful composers, just as there are few who have enough gift to become successful novelists or poets. But we do not deny the student the opportunity to learn to read and write English simply because we think he is not gifted enough to become a writer; on the contrary, we take great pains to teach him these things because we know that only by this means can he come to understand and appreciate great literature. If he has unusual gift enough to become a poet or novelist we are happy, to be sure, but we do not make him such by teaching him grammar. Likewise, there is no reason why everybody but tone-deaf persons should not study music technically; the greater insight one has into an art, the greater one's appreciation. And there is no doubt that cultivation of a technique gives greater insight into the works of the great masters than any other kind of study.

With these things in mind I have planned this book, based directly on the technique of the vocal sacred music of the sixteenth century. It is intended to be an introduction and guide to the early study of counterpoint, and deals with the construction of the single line and with the combination of two lines, three lines, and four lines. When he has thoroughly mastered the material presented here, however, the ambitious student should have acquired enough insight into contrapuntal technique to be able to go on with more advanced study, using a greater number of parts and continuing with instrumental counterpoint and fugue. This is possible because the study is based on music itself, all the rules being deduced from the actual practices of sixteenth-century composers. The principles they used have not been arbitrarily added to or subtracted from, and the student must make constant reference to their works.

The reason for the arbitrary choice of sacred music of the Golden Age as a basis of the present study may not be apparent at first thought. In fact, if we consider the study of counterpoint only as a basis for gaining technique in composition, we have to admit that, while modern music has many resemblances to that of the sixteenth century, there are modern compositions which resemble even more certain music before and after the Golden Age. There are many similarities, for instance, between Hindemith and Frescobaldi in respect to cross relations induced by lines tending in different directions; other similarities can be found between Stravinsky and the thirteenth and fourteenth centuries; one might even suggest that in regard to strictness of technique Schönberg has much in common with the school still known in old-fashioned music history books as the "dry-as-dust" school, that of Obrecht and Ockeghem. The truth is that the selection of any period for purposes of concentrated study is bound to be arbitrary. Bach has often served as a model, particularly in German counterpoint methods; and today certain composers, notably Hindemith, owe a tremendous debt to Bach. In rhythmic movement and in methods of musical construction the similarity between the new music and the old is no accident. The exclusion of Bach's music as a model in the present book does not mean that we are to consider Bach inferior as a contrapuntist. What we are trying to do is to find a period when the musical lines govern the harmonic progression; for this we must go back farther than Bach. In the eighteenth century, as I have pointed out before, the basic aspect is harmonic; and the lines, however excellent they may be, are usually generated from the harmonies.

The selection of the age of Palestrina is based on the compelling fact that here we have a period of music in which the lines do for the most part generate the harmonies, in which there is a consistent common practice[4] not too difficult to master, and in which we find remarkably little departure from that common practice. If Victoria can be readily distinguished from Palestrina, or Lassus from Victoria, it is on account of the greater frequency with which certain devices are used by one composer than by the other; the devices remain the same. Above all, counterpoint is a typical and consistent method of composition in this period.

The exclusion of the secular style, even of this period, is made on much the same basis: it is generally freer and more harmonic than the sacred style. Once the student has a firm grasp of the latter he should feel free to examine sacred and secular music both before and after the Golden Age; indeed, it is necessary that he should, so that he may avoid getting into a permanent technical rut. Until he has gained a keen sense of style, however, he must not deviate from the common practice of the style with which he is primarily concerned. It is one thing to depart from an established practice with full consciousness and

---

[4] By the term "common practice" are meant those devices and methods of composition which are the common property of a group of composers in any particular period. This common property is the norm, the strict adherence to which may at times be disregarded in small details by any one of such a group. In the Golden Age it can safely be said that Lassus, Victoria, and particularly Palestrina depart least from the common practice of the time; on account of their great consistency they are probably the best models that could be selected for beginners.

another to depart from it without realizing that anything has happened. Debussy's music, for instance, is full of consecutive fifths, but their use is one of the characteristic elements of his style; in our work consecutive fifths will only be slips, because they are not consistent with the style in question.

It may be said here that the study of counterpoint does not involve complete disregard for the chordal aspect in music. Although composers of the thirteenth century did not regularly have their melodies "harmonize" except at certain places, we find that the composers of the sixteenth century had a sophisticated taste in harmony within the frame of the modes. Their harmony was strictly regulated in regard to the vocabulary of chords that were used, but it did not dictate to the lines in regard to the construction of phrases as it did later.

The majority of the great modern collections of music in the long period up to and including Bach make use of the seven clefs. In this book all the excerpts have been transcribed into the bass and treble clefs. This became advisable when, in order to save space, certain excerpts were compressed into two staves. It also saves the beginning student the additional difficulty of having to decipher clefs unknown to him. In his own exercises, however, he should never write two musical lines on the same staff, and he should make the attempt early to use the different clefs. When he turns to the great editions for necessary further study he will have to learn them, else a vast literature will be closed to him. Besides this, a thorough knowledge of the clefs is essential for transposing music at sight, or for reading orchestral scores in which transposing instruments have a part.

The seven clefs fall into three categories: the G clef, the C clefs, and the F clefs. They are:

G on the second line, the treble clef:

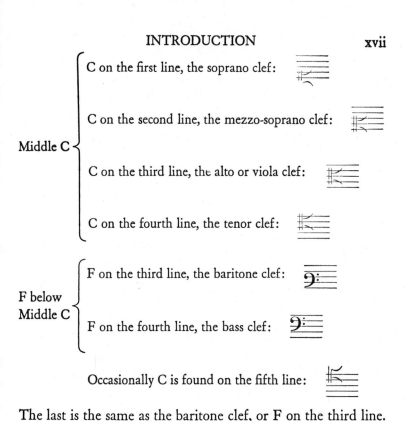

Middle C
- C on the first line, the soprano clef:
- C on the second line, the mezzo-soprano clef:
- C on the third line, the alto or viola clef:
- C on the fourth line, the tenor clef:

F below Middle C
- F on the third line, the baritone clef:
- F on the fourth line, the bass clef:

Occasionally C is found on the fifth line:

The last is the same as the baritone clef, or F on the third line. Any other variations in clefs can always be related to one of the seven above, for by means of some one of them any written note can be read anywhere in the octave.

It is fervently hoped that this study will be valuable to any student of counterpoint, regardless of his ultimate aims, and that it will give him not only the technical facility which the study of the species gives but also an understanding of the fundamentals of counterpoint which he could never get through the species — an appreciation, in short, of the fact that contrapuntal music is not necessarily harmony with figurations.

PART I

THE SINGLE LINE: PLAINSONG

THE SINGLE LINE: PLAINSONG

IN sixteenth-century music, line is of prime importance, for it is the generating force, the material from which the compositions themselves grow. In contrast with predominantly harmonic music, in which one line assumes the chief interest and forces all other lines — if there are distinguishable lines — to fall into the harmonic scheme which it generates, the polyphonic music we are to study is made up of interdependent lines, not absolutely free of each other but good individually, and at the same time accommodating themselves to an ensemble over which no one of them is unduly dictatorial.

Since we must lay stress on lines as such, it is almost indispensable to make a preliminary study of the individual line in order to obtain a clear idea of sixteenth-century polyphony. It stands to reason that unless one understands how to construct a good single line one has very little chance of understanding how to combine several lines. Moreover, for a time, at least, it is necessary for us to try to divorce ourselves from thinking in terms of vertical blocks or harmonies. For this purpose there is nothing better than the study of plainsong, the so-called Gregorian chants in the church modes. There is a tremendous literature of these compositions,[1] and they have the distinct advantage of being unaccompanied, so that their beauty of line can be studied without the distraction which is invariably created by supporting harmonies. Furthermore, these chants

---

[1] A very extensive collection of plainsong may be found in the *Liber Usualis* published by Desclée & Co. (Tournai, 1934) and available with introduction and rubrics in English at most good dealers in the United States. Smaller collections, but entirely adequate for the present purpose, are *Plainsong for Schools*, Part I (Liverpool: Rushworth & Draper, 1936) and *Kyriale seu Ordinarium Missae* (New York: J. Fischer & Bro., 1927).

offer an excellent introduction to the church modes in which
sixteenth-century sacred music is written.

The lines in most types of plainsong chants are magnificent
for their construction and their singable quality. Although the
chants are often accompanied by the organ nowadays, they
have not the slightest need for any accompaniment; they stand
perfectly by themselves, and in fact are more effective without
any support. It is mainly by becoming acquainted with them
in this fashion that one learns to appreciate how strong they
are and how satisfactory a single strand of melody can be.

In the earlier periods of contrapuntal music particularly,
these chants were often used as *canti firmi*. The composer cus-
tomarily placed one of them in one of the voice parts and wove
other lines of his own invention around it. This is undoubtedly
what gave the scholastic contrapuntists the idea of using *canti
firmi* in their little exercises. But the two practices have remarkably little in common. The exercises in scholastic counterpoint are painfully short and present no vital problems of
structure; as used by the contrapuntal composer, the cantus was
commonly the basis of a composition of at least several phrases.
Moreover, the cantus in a scholastic exercise is invariably regulated in prim rows of one note per measure, while in a motet
or movement of a Mass it is commonly treated with great
variety of rhythm. Although even in the sixteenth century the
use of such a cantus had become purely optional, the practice
of occasionally employing some sort of melody as the basis of a
contrapuntal composition has never completely died out. It
may be seen, for instance, in Bach's and Brahms's chorale
preludes and even nowadays in compositions like Hindemith's
Schwanendreher or *Mathis der Maler*.

The main purpose of our short study of plainsong is not to
learn to use the chants as *canti firmi* but rather to learn how to
construct good individual lines. The student must study as
many chants as he can lay his hands on, and *sing* them. He

should make a thorough technical analysis of them, and then write chants himself. In the long run it is principally through writing that he will acquire an intimate acquaintance with the modes, a critical power in regard to melodic line, and, not least of all, an appreciation of the subtleties of creating music in small forms.

THE MODES.[2] There are eight modes, known as the church modes, in which we ordinarily find the plainsong melodies. The note on which a chant ends — the *final* — and the range which it covers determine the mode of the melody. All chants fall into four basic classes of modes: the Dorian, the Phrygian, the Lydian, and the Mixolydian, according to whether they end on D, E, F, or G respectively, for these are the only finals ever to be used. (Transposed melodies will be discussed later in the chapter.) All chants have a possible range of an octave. This gives rise to another classification, for if the melody ranges upwards an octave from the final it is in an *authentic* mode; if it ranges upwards an octave from the note a fourth below the final it is in a corresponding *plagal* mode. This means that in the authentic modes the final lies at the bottom of the octave range, while in the plagal modes it lies almost in the middle of that range. Each of the four notes then, D, E, F, and G, does service as final not only for an authentic mode but also for a corresponding plagal mode, designated by the prefix "Hypo-."

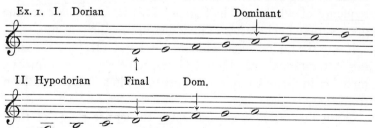

Ex. 1. I. Dorian   Dominant

II. Hypodorian   Final   Dom.

[2] For a fuller discussion of the modes, see J. F. Arnold, *Plainsong Accompaniment* (London: Oxford University Press, 1927).

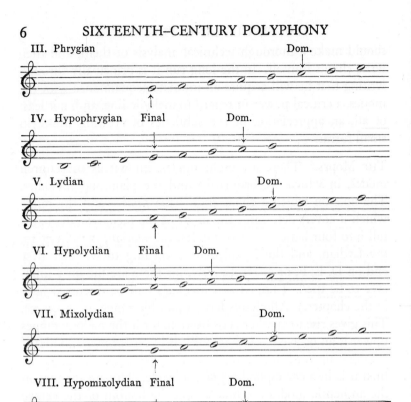

Since no accidentals are used when the scale, or mode, is pure, the first thing one notices is that each mode has a characteristic sequence of whole and half steps. This in itself indicates the great variety in character in melodies in the different modes.

It must be noticed that, while Modes I and VIII have the same range, their finals are D and G respectively; in consequence, melodies in the one mode are constructed in a different fashion from those in the other.

Often the melodies do not cover the entire range of their octave. Some of them are remarkable for their restraint in this respect. However, they can and sometimes do range a note above the octave limit, and it is very common for them to go a note below that limit. It is common to classify a chant which does not range more than a fifth or even a sixth above the final as being in a plagal mode, even if it does not cover the entire lower range.

In plainsong melodies there are certain notes in the mode which are of particular importance — often of more importance than the final so far as the frequence of their occurrence is concerned. One of the most important of all is the dominant, since it is often the note around which the melody revolves, particularly in the psalm tones. In the authentic modes it lies a fifth above the final unless that fifth happens to fall on B, in which case C is substituted. In the plagal modes it is a third below the dominant of the corresponding authentic modes, unless again it falls on B, in which case C is again substituted. B is never used as a dominant.

It will suffice here to give only the range of the different modes and their dominants and mediants.

Mode	Range	Final	Dominant	Mediant
I	D — D	D	A	F
II	A — A	D	F	E
III	E — E	E	C	G
IV	B — B	E	A	G
V	F — F	F	C	A
VI	C — C	F	A	D
VII	G — G	G	D	C
VIII	D — D	G	C	A

In the type of chants which we shall examine in this preliminary study the student will be mainly interested in knowing on what notes melodies may begin in the different modes and on what notes phrases other than final ones may end. This, together with information concerning other notes which play more or less important roles in the various modes, may be found

in a table in the article by W. S. Rockstro entitled "Ecclesiastical Modes" in *Grove's Dictionary of Music and Musicians.*

RHYTHM. Although the problem of plainsong rhythm has in
the past been a very fertile field for disagreement, the interpretation of the Solesmes monks, who have spent many years
in research on the subject, is the one most generally accepted
today. A common statement that plainsong melodies have no
rhythm is entirely misleading; they do have a very subtle
rhythm. What they lack, and rightly so, is a pulsation in
metrical fashion. In respect to rhythm they differ markedly
from secular music such as folk songs or dances. The physical
attraction of pulsation in these latter pieces is one of their inherent characteristics, but in plainsong pulsation would only
tend to distract attention from the mental attitude of worship
which these chants strive to heighten; it is not their purpose to
call attention to themselves or to excite physical response as the
dance melody does.

The main principle of plainsong rhythm is to give to the
syllables of the text that stress or lack of stress which they have
in speech. Plainsong *is* musical speech, and its rhythm actually
arises out of the natural rhythm of the Latin words to which it
has been set. This can be illustrated by the following version of
the Credo. The music is ordinarily not barred in the course of
phrases, for barring it in any way would tend to create in the
minds of the singers a rigidity of beat which it actually lacks.
It is a freely sung music and must not adhere to a rigid underlying pulsation. In order to illustrate how the stresses are placed,
however, we might bar it as in Ex. 2, the only manner in which
barring could be effective even in a slight way.

Though in this version the music is too rigid, nevertheless the
basic stresses are illustrated, and it is easy to see that the music
is not metrical in the manner of dance music or, for that matter,
most music after the seventeenth century. In rhythm it much

more resembles certain modern music where the measures are uneven and the accents are so arranged that they do not recur regularly.

Ex. 2

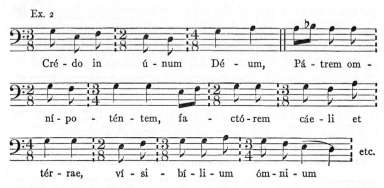

Cré - do in ú - num Dé - um, Pá - trem om -
ní - po - tén - tem, fa - ctó - rem cáe - li et
tér - rae, ví - si - bí - li - um óm - ni - um

Such uneven arrangements of rhythms are as common in the more ornamented plainsong melodies as in the syllabic type above. The beginning of the Kyrie of the *Lux et origo* Mass might be barred thus:

Ex. 3.

Ký - ri - e e - lé - i - son

When the student begins to write plainsong melodies he should never bar them in the manner illustrated in these examples. These barred illustrations are intended only to call his attention to the fact that the <u>melodies must not be metrical, that they must be rhythmically free.</u> This same underlying point of view will arise again in connection with the polyphonic music we are going to study, and the student will see that precisely the same principles are involved there as here.

<u>MELODIC INTERVALS.</u> Plainsong melodies move predominantly <u>stepwise</u>, although skips are frequently introduced to give them

variety and to keep them from becoming uninteresting scale passages. All melodic intervals — chromatic, diminished, and augmented ones excepted — up to and including the minor sixth are used, and the leap of the octave is occasionally found. The vocabulary of intervals then consists of major and minor seconds, major and minor thirds, perfect fourths and fifths, minor sixths, and perfect octaves. All other intervals are found so rarely as to exclude them from a list of those commonly used. Intervals outside this vocabulary are sometimes found between the last note of one section of a chant and the first note of the following section, but never in the course of a phrase.

Ex. 4.   Kyrie from *Alme Pater* Mass

e - le - i - son. Ky - ri - e

The larger leaps seem to occur most often near the beginning of a phrase, although this is not invariably true.

Ex. 5.   Sanctus (V) † *Dorian*   Kyrie (XI)   *Dorian(?)*

Kyrie (XI)   *Dorian(?)*   Gloria (XI)   *Dorian*

Rarely do more than two skips in the same direction take place successively, and when even two occur they are usually ascending minor thirds, as shown in Ex. 6.

† The Roman numerals given in parentheses refer to the Masses as they are listed in the *Liber Usualis*.

Ex. 6. Kyrie (II)

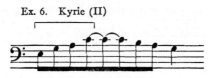

Sometimes a rising fifth is followed by a minor third in the same direction:

Ex. 7. Sanctus (II)

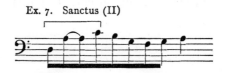

In such cases it is customary to repeat or lengthen the value of the upper note of the first interval before proceeding to the still higher note. Many times the upper note, after the leap of the fifth, sinks downward before making the additional leap of the third:

Ex. 8. Kyrie (IV)

A figure outlining a triad is not uncommon at the beginning of phrases:

Ex. 9. Agnus (IV)   Agnus (XVII)

Kyrie (X)

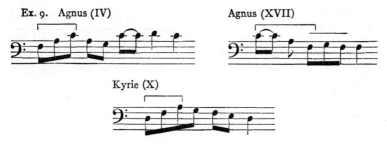

But it must be used with discretion, for if it recurs too frequently it causes a "tonality" which is foreign to most plainsong chants. The figures

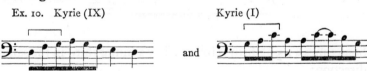

Ex. 10.   Kyrie (IX)   Kyrie (I)

and

are far from unusual as the initial notes of phrases. The figure

Ex. 11.

or

is uncommon, and

Ex. 12.

is practically never found. Once in a while there are melodies which give an initial impression of being constructed on a pentatonic or five-note scale:

Ex. 13.   Gloria (III)

but which proceed in a fashion that tends to obliterate the first impression.

Great care must be exercised at all times in the treatment of the augmented fourth, the tritone, which occurs between the notes F and B. The direct leap upwards or downwards over this interval is never to be found. The nearest approach to it is the figure

Ex. 14

which does occur sometimes. However, this motive is never used in a cadence or at the beginning of a phrase. When it is used in the course of a phrase the B and the F should not be exposed at both the upper and lower points of the melodic line, as in

Ex. 15

or

but should be sheathed, at least partly, as in the phrase "Christe" in the Kyrie I of the *Lux et origo* Mass:

Ex. 16

or in the phrase of the Kyrie I of the *Kyrie fons bonitatis* Mass, where the interval is used in a scale passage:

Ex. 17

In both cases B is preceded by the C above and is thus not exposed.

It is impossible to give here anything like a complete table of figures of leaps to be found in these melodies, but as the student gains familiarity with plainsong he will recognize those figures which are common and most effective. In general, it may be said that a leap is most often followed by a turning in the opposite direction; and the greater the leap the more important this becomes if one is to avoid a feeling of melodic disjointed-

same general rules followed by Palestrina in his polyphony.

ness. A skip in one direction may be followed by a skip in the opposite direction:

Ex. 18. Sanctus (IV)   Sanctus (VIII)

Ite missa est (VIII)

or it may be — and more often is — preceded and followed by a stepwise movement in the opposite direction:

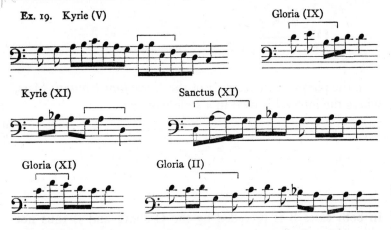

Ex. 19. Kyrie (V)   Gloria (IX)

Kyrie (XI)   Sanctus (XI)

Gloria (XI)   Gloria (II)

It must be remembered that, as we have said, plainsong chants move mostly by step.

DIRECTION. Most phrases have a tendency to take a descending course. They often begin relatively high, and by a series of gently undulating waves sink gradually to the final. In certain modes particularly, they may even descend a note below the final before they come back to it to close. If a melody does not

begin high, it frequently makes a steep ascent near the beginning, so that the effect is much the same as if it had begun high.
In almost no case is the final reached immediately after an
ascent from a low point. Characteristic types of lines may be
seen in the examples of chants in the different modes quoted on
pages 22–28.

Melodic sequences are rarely found in plainsong chants. One
often finds repetitions of figures or, oftener still, repetitions with
small variations; but successive and orderly transposition of
figures from one degree to another is almost unknown.

CADENCES. It has already been said that the final is one of the
two factors that determine in what mode a melody is written;
the other, range, determines whether a chant is in an authentic
mode or its corresponding plagal mode. There seems to be no
difference in cadential formulae between the corresponding
authentic and plagal modes. The most important thing to
remember is that the final must be approached in good fashion
if the melody is to give the flavor of the mode in which it is
written, and that one of the most characteristic ways of doing
this is to capitalize on the difference in the sizes of the intervals
which lie above and below the final. A point that cannot be
overstressed is the fact that the intervallic relationship between
the final and the notes above and below it is different in each
of the modes. For example, let us take D, the final of the
Dorian modes. The note C is a whole step below, E a whole
step above, and F a minor third above. In the Phrygian modes,

Ex. 20.

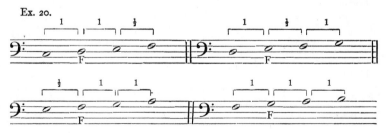

where E is the final, these relationships are different: D lies a whole step below, F a half step above, and G a minor third above. In the Lydian and Mixolydian modes these relationships differ again.

The flavor of a mode depends a great deal upon the use of these notes in the cadence. In the Dorian, Phrygian, and Mixolydian modes the note below the final plays a particularly important part. In those modes it is very commonly used as a penultimate note, and if it does not immediately precede the final it is usually not separated from it by many other notes. In the Lydian modes the note below the final is comparatively rarely used in the cadence. It comes into constant use first in polyphonic music.

When F is used as a penultimate note in chants in the Mixolydian mode, B is ordinarily avoided in the line leading directly to it. The two notes used in close proximity give the tritone, which is always a poor interval and hard both to think and to sing.

Considering the fact that the four notes just discussed are so often used, there are a surprising number of ways of forming cadences in the different modes. A few typical cadences are the following:

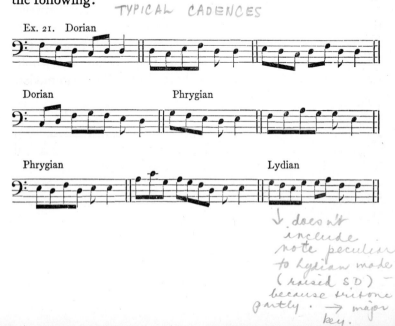

Ex. 21. Dorian

Dorian   Phrygian

Phrygian   Lydian

avoids L. N. → Tonic progression.

Lydian

Mixolydian

ACCIDENTALS. The flat is the only accidental ever found in plain-song melodies, and it is used only to alter the note B. This is attributable in the first place to the tritonal relationship between F and B, an interval which has always caused embarrassment in melodic lines; when B is flatted the two notes can proceed one to the other perfectly safely. In the second place, it is often much easier to sing a minor second than a major one. This

becomes obvious in such figures as

where the melody rises from D to A, goes a second above, and sinks again to A. After a rise of a fifth the difference between a major second formed by the notes A, B, A and a minor second formed by the notes A, B♭, A is very appreciable. And when this figure occurs — as it so often does, particularly in the Dorian mode — the B is practically always flatted.

There is not usually much occasion to make use of the B♭ in the Phrygian modes, particularly in figures which rise from the E itself. However, the figure D A B♭ A discussed in the para-graph above is not rare in the Phrygian, and when it is used the B is ordinarily flatted.

In the Lydian modes the B is very often flatted to avoid the tritone between the final and the fourth above it. In a great number of Lydian chants this alteration takes place constantly, and as a result the chants have the flavor of the major mode. (For a good example of this, see the Kyrie of the *De angelis* Mass.)

In the Mixolydian modes it is very uncommon to find B♭. B natural, which forms a major third with the final, is one of the characteristic notes of the mode, and if it is altered often the scale ceases to be Mixolydian and becomes Dorian.

TRANSPOSITION. Although the use of the flat as an accidental is comparatively common, the transposition of melodies up a fifth accomplishes the same result without the accidental. And such transposition of melodies, particularly in the Dorian and Phrygian modes, is not rare. Once in a while Lydian melodies are so transposed; but Mixolydian melodies are never so treated, since such transposition alters the third above the final. An example of transposition up a fifth can be seen in the Benedictus of the *Lux et origo* Mass. I shall not quote the whole chant, but only a phrase which illustrates the effect of such transposition. Though this is not the final phrase, the last note of it is actually the written final of the chant.

Ex. 22

Be - ne - díc - tus qui vé - nit   in   nó - mi - ne   Dó - mi - ne

The chant is in the Hypophrygian mode, whose final is E. Here in the transposed version, however, the final is B, and the fifth above it which is sung to the syllable "dic" is F. If the chant were not transposed and the interval relationships in the scale were to remain the same as they are here this note would have to be B♭.

Besides transposition of melodies up a fifth we find sometimes, although much more rarely, transposition up a fourth. This has the effect of gaining automatically the accidental F♯. We have seen that B♭ is often actually written in the plainsong melodies. But F♯ as such is never used, and the only way of securing the effect of it is by means of this transposition. Ordi-

narily the only melodies to be so transposed are those in the
Phrygian modes. Curiously enough, however, this treatment
deprives these modes of one of their most characteristic intervals — the minor second above the final, which occurs only in
them. This fact undoubtedly goes a long way to explain why
so few of the Phrygian melodies are written with A as a final.
The following antiphon is a good example, however, of the
process.

Ex. 23

Lae-tén-tur cáe - li, et ex -súl - tet   tér - ra   an - te fá - ci - em

Dó - mi - ni,   quó - ni -am vé - nit.

FORMS. In view of the fact that the present study is only a preliminary to the main business of counterpoint, and makes no
attempt to explore deeply the intricacies of the subject of plainsong, it will suffice the student to analyze only certain types of
chants. The Kyrie is one of the most convenient chants for the
purpose, for its numerous settings are characterized by great
variety of form, mode, and melodic treatment. It is composed
of three main divisions based on a text consisting of three
phrases: "Kyrie eleison," which is sung three times; "Christe
eleison," which is sung three times; and again "Kyrie eleison,"
which is sung three times. The whole movement is made up,
therefore, of nine distinct phrases of text.

The simplest musical form is that in which the repetition of
text in each of the three parts is echoed literally in the melody.
This is illustrated by the Kyrie of the Mass *Kyrie magnae Deus
potentiae* (Ex. 24).

At the end of the Kyrie I is the sign *iij*, indicating that the

phrase is to be sung three times before going on to the Christe.
The same intention is indicated at the end of the phrase,
"Christe eleison," and again at the close of the Kyrie II. In this
particular Kyrie the musical unity of the movement is further
emphasized by the fact that the melody of the Kyrie II is ex-

Ex. 24.   *Kyrie* (V)

exactly the same as that of the Kyrie I. It is perhaps hardly necessary to remark that, unless it is very skillful, this type of
treatment runs the risk of making the movement sound
monotonous.

A slight variation of this procedure is illustrated in the Kyrie
of the *Lux et origo* Mass.[3] Here the melody of the Kyrie I is
each time the same, and the melody of the Christe likewise
repeats itself. In the Kyrie II, however, there is a new melody
which is sung twice the same, as is indicated by the *ij* at the end
of the phrase, but which is changed a little the third time by the
addition of three notes at the beginning of the phrase. The fact
that the melodies of the Kyrie I and Kyrie II are not the same

[3] See p. 28.

adds a certain interest; and even though the three phrases of
the Kyrie II are almost identical, the three new notes before the
last phrase give it a freshness that it would lack without them.

The various Kyries range in musical complexity from the
simple ones just discussed up to much more elaborate ones,
such as the famous "Cum jubilo" Kyrie.[4] In this chant not a
single phrase is followed immediately by a literal repetition.
On the other hand, it is beautifully handled musically, and
there are plenty of recurrences of musical ideas. In the Kyrie I
not only are the first and third phrases identical, but the second
phrase differs from them only in the notes to which the first
two syllables of the word "Kyrie" are sung. The first and third
phrases of the Christe are identical and cadence on the dominant,
while the second phrase corresponds with the first phrase in the
Kyrie I in all but the introductory three notes, which are a small
variation of the first four notes of the original phrase. The first
and third phrases of the Kyrie II are identical for the first four-
teen notes, but from here on they differ; the first borrows its
cadence from the first phrase of the Christe, and the third, after
a literal repetition of the intonation,[5] borrows the whole of the
second phrase in the Christe section. The second phrase in the
Kyrie II corresponds exactly to the second phrase of the Christe.
It is interesting to note that there are only two kinds of
cadences in the whole movement: the first ends phrases 1, 2, 3,
5, 8, and 9; the second ends phrases 4, 6, and 7. As to beginnings
of phrases, 1 and 3 are alike; 2 is unique; 4 and 6 are the same;
5 and 8 are the same; and 7 and 9 are the same. A most important aspect of this Kyrie is the rise in intensity which occurs as
the chant proceeds. In the Kyrie I, A is the highest note; in the
Christe, the line rises to B♭; in the Kyrie II, the climax is reached
on D an octave above the final of the chant. But, except in the

[4] See pp. 22–23.
[5] The intonation of a plainsong melody is that portion at the beginning of
the chant, up to the asterisk, which is sung, or intoned, by the priest alone.
After the asterisk, the chant is carried on by the rest of the singers in unison.

case of the first and third phrases in the Christe section, the lines flow typically downwards.

Below, an example of a chant in each mode is quoted. These chants are intended to serve only as an introduction, and the student should supplement his examination of them by the study of as many more as he can. He will then be able to choose the ones he wishes to use as models for chants of his own composition.

Ex. 25. *Orbis factor* (XI) Dorian

1. Ky - ri - e   *   e - - - - - le - i - son. *iij*

Chri - ste   e - - - - - le - i - son. *iij.*

Ky - ri - e   e - - - - - le - i - son. *ij.*

Ky - ri - e   *   e - - - - le - i - son.

(see p. 21) Ex. 26. *Cum jubilo* (IX) Hypodorian

1. Ky - ri - e   *   e - le - i - son.

Ky - ri - e   e - le - i - son.

Ky - ri - e   e - le - i - son.

Chri - ste   e - le - i - son. Chri - ste

e - le - i - son.   Chri - ste

e - le - i - son.   Ky - ri - e

e - le - i - son.   Ky - ri - e

e - le - i - son.   Ky - ri - e

*   **

e - le - i - son.

Ex. 27. *Pater cuncta* † (XII)   Hypodorian

2.   San - ctus, San - ctus, San - ctus

Do - mi - nus De - us Sa - ba - oth. Ple - ni sunt cae - li et ter - ra

† In the Ordinary of the Mass there is no Kyrie in the second mode. The
Sanctus here quoted will, however, show the characteristics of the mode.

glo - ri - a   tu - a. Ho - san - na in ex - cel - - - sis.

Be - ne - di - ctus qui ve - nit   in   no - mi - ne   Do - mi - ni.

Ho - san - na   in   ex - cel - - - - - sis.

Ex. 28. *Kyrie fons bonitatis* (II)

3.

Ky - ri - e

e - le - i - son. *iij.* Chri - ste

e - le - - i - son. *iij.* Ky - ri - e

e - le - i - son. *ij.*

Ky - ri - e

e - le - i - son.

Ex. 29. *Kyrie Deus sempiterne* (III)   Hypophrygian

Ex. 30. *De Angelis* (VIII) Lydian (almost major)

5. Ky-ri - e   *   e   -   le -i-son. *iij.*

Chri-ste   e   -   le - i-son. *iij.*

Ky-ri - e   e   -   le - i-son. *ij.*

Ky-ri - e   *   **

` e   -   -   -   le - i - son.

Ex. 31. *Vel, ubi moris est* (XVII) Hypolydian

6. Ky - ri - e   *   e   -   -   -   le - i - son. *iij.*

Chri - ste   e   -   -   le - i - son. *iij.*

Ky-ri - e   e   -   -   le - i - son. *ij.*

Ky - ri - e   *   e - -

-    -   le - i - son.

Ex. 32. *Conditor Kyrie omnium* Mixolydian

7.

Ky - ri - e

*

e - le - i - son. Ky - ri - e

e - - le - i - son. Ky - ri - e

e - le - i - son. Chri - ste

e - le - i - son.

Chri - ste e - - le - i - son.

Chri - ste e - le - i - son.

Ky - ri - e e - le - i - son.

Ky - ri - e

e - le - i - son. Ky - ri - e

e - le - i - son.

Ex. 33. *Lux et origo* (I)   Hypomixolydian

8.

Ky - ri - e   e - le - i - son. *iij.*

Chri - ste   e - - -

le - i - son. *iij.* Ky - - ri - e

e - - le - i - son. *ij.* Ky - ri - e

e - - le - i - son.

PART II

ANALYSIS OF CONTRAPUNTAL TECHNIQUE

ANALYSIS OF CONTRAPUNTAL TECHNIQUE

I. THE MODES. In plainsong only eight modes were used; in the contrapuntal music which is to form the basis of our study we find that number increased by four: two authentic and two plagal. These new modes are:

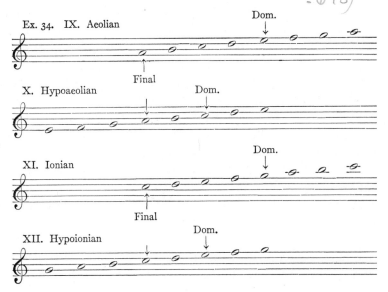

Ex. 34. IX. Aeolian

Dom.

Final

X. Hypoaeolian

Dom.

XI. Ionian

Dom.

Final

XII. Hypoionian

Dom.

The authentic and plagal modes with B as final were called the Locrian and the Hypolocrian, but on account of the diminished fifth above the final, which prevented a satisfactory cadence, they were never used; they were merely theoretical modes.

Although the number of modes used in contrapuntal music was thus theoretically as many as twelve, we find in actual practice that there were considerably fewer than that. In the first place, there is not an appreciable number of compositions in the

fifth and sixth — the Lydian and Hypolydian — modes. These
two with F as the final tended to be swallowed up by the Ionian
modes. This came about because of the tremendous importance
which lay in the triad on the fourth degree of all the modes.
Naturally, this triad always had to be either major or minor,
never diminished, and in the Lydian modes it could only be
changed from diminished to major by flatting the B. But once
it became customary to flat the B these two modes lost the
characteristics which distinguished them from the Ionian modes.
Therefore pieces which end on F as a final usually have B♭ in
their signatures, which automatically puts them in the transposed Ionian modes. In the second place, the number of modes
regularly in use was reduced by the fact that there came to be
less and less difference between the authentic and the plagal
modes. In contrapuntal music of this period the range of any
one voice is rarely much greater than an octave, so that each
part stays within its own mode. But this raises the question of
how to determine what mode a part-composition as a whole is
in. Any two adjacent voices, of course, are bound to have their
ranges about a fifth apart. The alto, for example, ordinarily
ranges about a fifth below the soprano; the tenor has a range
of about the same distance below the alto, and the bass about the
same distance again below the tenor. As a result, the soprano
and tenor have ranges about an octave apart and consequently
in the same mode, while the alto and bass have their ranges
about an octave from each other and in the same mode. Logically this means that if the tenor and soprano sing in an authentic mode the bass and alto will sing in a plagal mode, or vice
versa.

The usual method of determining the mode of a part-
composition is based upon two things. First, the note on which
the lowest voice ends is always the final. Second, it is the compass of the tenor which decides whether the composition is to
be considered authentic or plagal. This is based on a tradition

that dates back to the early days of polyphonic music, when the
tenor carried the plainsong melody around which the rest of
the composition was built. In the sixteenth century, however,
it is often difficult or impossible to tell whether a composition
is to be considered authentic or plagal. If there is no tenor part,
or if the piece is not based on a plainsong melody, or if the
plainsong melody on which it is based is equally important in all
the voices, it becomes almost impossible to tell.

From the practical standpoint, therefore, we may consider
that the number of modes in regular use which have real dis-
tinction from each other is actually five: the DORIAN, the
PHRYGIAN, the MIXOLYDIAN, the AEOLIAN, and the IONIAN.

2. TRANSPOSITION. As in the case of plainsong melodies, the compositions of the sixteenth century may be transposed. But if
they are, it is always upwards a fourth or downwards a fifth, and
it always entails the use of B♭ in the signature of each part. This
transposition was not for purposes of pitch, since music of this
period was not conceived in terms of absolute pitch, and singers
were free to sing where it was most comfortable for the voices
and where it sounded best. Neither was it for the purpose of
automatically gaining accidentals, as was the case in the transposition of plainsong melodies. It was more likely for the sake
of convenience in writing all the parts on their respective staves
without having to use leger lines. This transposition is the only
one found regularly throughout the sixteenth century; the transposition to other degrees with the use of more accidentals in the
signature became common only in and after the seventeenth
century.

3. ACCIDENTALS. In the course of a composition certain accidentals
were often used. Most of them resulted from the custom of always ending a piece with a major triad (or without any third
in the chord at all) rather than with a minor one, regardless of

1. tièrce de picardie
2. Raised leading note

the mode in which the piece was written. In addition, whenever the penultimate chord was based on the fifth above the
final, it likewise was ordinarily major. *really amounts to sharpening the leading note*

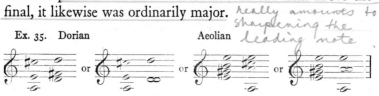

Ex. 35.   Dorian   Aeolian

These practices served to introduce F♯, C♯, and G♯ into the
modal system. Furthermore, B♭ had been in common usage in
plainsong and had even made its way into the signatures of
polyphonic compositions. Its use as an accidental naturally
necessitated the introduction of E♭ whenever a piece was transposed. For example, if a composition in which one of the voices
had the figure

Ex. 36

were transposed upwards a fourth, the notation had to be

Ex. 37

These five accidentals, B♭, E♭, F♯, C♯, and G♯, are the only ones
that were regularly used during the Golden Age.[1] Moreover,
they were never used as enharmonic notations of A♯, D♯, G♭,
D♭, or A♭, since the tempered scale was not yet in use.

[1] Let it be borne in mind that we are concerned here with the common
practice of the Golden Age. Exceptions to the statement above may be found
in abundance in such compositions as the madrigals of Gesualdo and some
of the early motets of Lassus; even in Palestrina's sacred works examples of
exceptions may occasionally be found: see, for instance, the extraordinary use
of D♯ in the five-voice motet, *Peccantem me quotidie.*

4. RHYTHM. Sixteenth-century music is as outstanding on account of the elasticity and diversity of its rhythms as it is on account of its singable intervals. The ease and grace with which it moves rhythmically are astonishing to one who knows only eighteenth- and nineteenth-century music. At times, however, composers of the twentieth century move with the magnificent freedom of sixteenth- and seventeenth-century composers. This freedom in both the old music and the new lies not only in the rhythm of the ensemble but also in the rhythmic diversity that the various individual voices have in contrast with each other.

It will be recalled that this principle of freedom was the underlying basis for the rhythm of the plainsong melodies discussed in Part I. In barring plainsong melodies as we did, far too great a rigidity was implied. In polyphonic compositions, on the other hand, the pulsation must be more exact, since music which is in more than one part is bound to have a vertical aspect. Contrapuntal melodies must flow along easily, but they cannot ignore each other rhythmically or the ensemble would be chaotic. Moreover, the individual parts could not be readily distinguished. Even the earliest contrapuntists realized this.

There are two more or less well-defined types of ensemble composition that are commonly employed: (1) familiar style, =homophonic or the movement of all the voices in the same rhythm, which produces a chord-like progression,[2] and (2) fugal style, or the =polyphonic independent movement of the individual voices rhythmically and in imitative fashion.[3] Neither of these types is always pursued doggedly from one end of the composition to the other; one often finds them contrasted or combined in the same composition. Furthermore, pieces are often written as a whole or in part in a style that partakes of both the familiar and the fugal styles. Though these pieces may not contain any imitation as

[2] See the beginning of Palestrina's *Stabat Mater*, quoted on p. 40.
[3] See Palestrina's *In diebus illis*, quoted on p. 169.

such, at the same time the different voices move along with rhythmic independence.

An underlying pulsation regulates the movement of all the voices, regardless of how great their number. The half note is the ordinary rhythmic unit. (In most modern popular editions of this music the editors have halved the note values and made the quarter note the rhythmic unit. This in no way alters the music in regard to speed of performance, for the proportions of the note values remain the same.) When the half note is the unit we find double whole notes, whole notes, half notes, quarter notes, and eighth notes. No note smaller than the eighth is ever used in such a case.

Ex. 38

Very seldom does a melody move along for any length of time in notes of the same value. The sixteenth century is remarkable for its understanding of the principle that a large part of the beauty of any melody is created not only by its intervals but also by its rhythmic variety. It is hard indeed to find more than two eighths in succession, and successive quarter notes never continue long. (Too many are very liable to produce a rhythmically flabby melody.) In compositions of two or three parts, however, there is greater freedom in the use of quarter notes in succession than in compositions of more parts. In the fifth section of Lassus' third *Penitential Psalm*, for example, we find the following melodies:

Ex. 39

This is due to the fact that in two-part compositions the composer is faced with an inherent minimum of resources in
respect to the ensemble, and in order to keep the piece from
plodding along in whole and half notes he sometimes uses a
greater number of quarters than he would if he were writing
for more voices. Yet even the great number of successive
quarters we have just seen is rare in sacred music, and it would
be difficult to find very many examples like this one.

In the tenth section of the same psalm, written for three
voices, we find the following:

Ex. 40

In the eighth section, written for four voices, we find:

Ex. 41

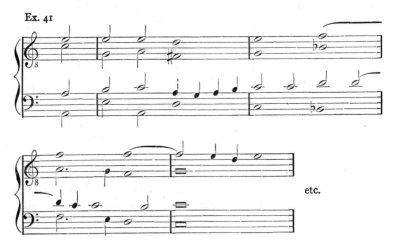

etc.

It is significant that the use of quarters becomes progressively more restrained as the number of voices increases. If all the voices in the last example ran on in the same fashion as those in the first the ensemble effect would be lacking in clarity and too "unbuttoned" for ordinary purposes. It is the rhythmic contrast of the voices that gives them individuality and makes them stand out from each other.

If a composer must not let a melody run on too long in quarters, he must on the other hand not let it plod along in half or whole notes unless there is a special reason, such as using a plainsong melody as a *cantus firmus* in whole notes. If such a special reason does not exist, a plodding melody simply sounds stodgy. One of the great secrets of fine melodies is rhythmic contrast within the line, but even this matter must be regulated according to the number of voices in the composition and according to the spirit of the text which is to be set.

In order to see how sixteenth-century composers liked to

handle rhythms, let us begin by examining a secular composition, the simple two-part verse which follows the introductory
refrain of Claude le Jeune's *Revecy venir du Printemps*.

Ex. 42

This piece is of a type of music written on what were known
in France at the time as *vers mesurés*. The rhythms of the notes
were made to correspond with the poetic rhythms of the words
to which they were set, and the result is that the compositions
sound so fresh and bound along so lightly that they are completely captivating. In the sixteenth century bar lines were
either not written at all in vocal music or were written very
infrequently, usually only to indicate closes or ends of phrases.
There is an absence of bar lines even in the modern edition of
Revecy venir du Printemps. Indeed, it would be difficult to
write them with any regularity, for the rhythm changes almost

constantly and would necessitate an alternation between meas-

ures of $\frac{4}{4}$, $\frac{3}{4}$, and $\frac{3}{2}$:

Ex. 43

The time signatures would look almost like those in the last movement of Stravinsky's *Sacre du Printemps*. It is interesting to observe, by the way, that the point of view in these two works is very much the same so far as rhythm is concerned, although they are separated so widely in time.

Another example, this time almost directly opposed to the le Jeune in the spirit of both words and music, is the magnificent

Ex. 44

Stabat Mater of Palestrina. Basically we find in this sacred composition the same freedom of movement that we found in le Jeune's secular piece. It is mostly in familiar style and is particularly effective on account of its antiphonal arrangement.

Here the printed bar lines are in many cases only a fiction. The first phrase does not move along in ordinary duple meter, but, giving a beat to each half note, thus:

Ex. 45

and the answering phrase in the second chorus cuts rhythmically across the bar lines:

Ex. 46

It is most interesting to note that, although the last two syllables of the word "lacrymosa" occupy four full beats, the first chorus enters before the second chorus has completely finished, so that there is an overlapping of rhythms (see Ex. 47). Rhythmic variation such as this is to be found in music of all types in this period. Rarely does any sort of sixteenth-century music move in the monotonous metrical fashion typical of the eighteenth century or in the languishing and at times amorphous fashion of much nineteenth-century music.

Ex. 47

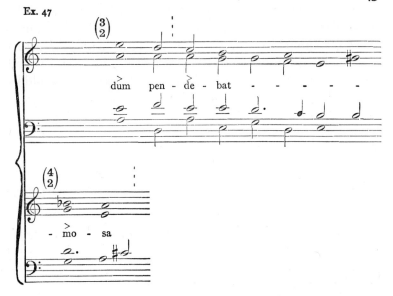

There is no denying that the ensemble in compositions written in fugal style most often moves in somewhat decided duple, and in some cases triple, meter. And the more complicated the rhythms of the individual lines become in contrast to each other, the more true this seems to be. Take, for example, Palestrina's *Lapidabant Stephanum*,[4] which is a fugal type of composition, each voice entering separately (Ex. 48).

First, taking the ensemble as such, nobody would deny that it moves in measures of four beats, a beat to each half note. This feeling is created mostly by the way the dissonances are treated, particularly the suspensions. But when one looks at the individual voices one finds that the accents very often fail to agree with the bar lines. In performance, of course, these

[4] Except in cases where cited examples are identified as psalms, movements of the Mass, or other types of compositions, all illustrations with titles are motets, whose sources may be found in the table, "Sources of Illustrations," p. 211.

accents must not be beaten out obviously, but they must be recognized clearly in the minds of the performers, or the music means nothing rhythmically. On the other hand, the actual barring of each individual voice according to its accents would lead in many cases to a distressingly complex score. It would be

Ex. 48

almost impossible for the reader to grasp it quickly, and it would be most difficult to conduct or to sing under a conductor. Such procedure would only stress a point that is already obvious to those who understand the rhythmic basis of the music of this period.

In music of any period there are certain things that give notes accent: (1) Long notes tend to be more strongly accented than short ones, a fact which can easily be illustrated by the example from le Jeune. (2) Leaping to or from a note often tends to accent it, and this is emphasized when the note is of longer duration than its neighbors. (3) Extremity in range is often effective in influencing accentuation; for example, a note at the top of an ascent or at the bottom of a descent will ordinarily tend to gain accent and to stand out because of its location. And (4) the accents in the words to which the notes are set often give accents to the notes themselves. In the sixteenth century duration of notes and stress on syllables in the text are the main factors in accenting; and generally (though not always) longer notes are given to accented syllables of words.

Long notes — with the exception of those which come in cadences at the ends of lines — ordinarily tend to create tension,
and short notes to relax it. Greater tension is usually found on
the stronger beats, especially when the long notes are forced
into a dissonant position by other notes moving against them;
energy is stored up in this position and is spent on the weak
beats. This is why a melody running along for a considerable
distance in notes of small value tends to sound flabby; it does
not store up the energy it spends.

In the models we are examining there are more or less definite situations in which we find notes of different values; and,
while it would be difficult to formulate a set of rules that would
cover all possible situations relating to the adjustment of
rhythms within the measure, some general suggestions can be
made in connection with all the types of notes used. It must
be kept in mind that the meter and general pace of the ensemble
very frequently disagree with the rhythms in the individual
voices.

Our models usually begin with comparatively long notes —
whole notes or double whole notes; it is only after the pieces
are on their way that shorter notes begin to creep in. This is
bound to be more evident in sacred music than in secular, since
its pace is so much more dignified and restrained, and since it
never lilts along except in the case of "alleluia" sections which
sometimes serve to wind up the motet.

1. Double whole notes are practically always used in all voices
at the close of a composition — that is, in the last measure, which
they fill. They often serve also as the initial note of entering
voices, particularly at the beginning of a composition. They
rarely occur in the course of an individual line, where they
would only stop the flow, but they often serve as a note of repose at the close of the line.

Ex. 49.   Palestrina, *Exaudi Domine*

2. Whole notes may also be used as initial and final notes in an individual line (except in the final cadence); and they may occur in the course of a phrase as well. As in the case of all types of notes, they must not plod along one after the other for any length of time.

Ex. 50.   Palestrina, *Lauda Sion*

3. Half notes are the most frequently used of all notes. In the first place they are the common unit of movement in this music. They serve comparatively rarely as initial notes of a composition in sacred style, but in the course of the composition they are freely used as initial notes of phrases in individual lines. They do not commonly figure on a weak beat as final

notes of a line or phrase, unless it is followed immediately by the beginning of another phrase in the same voice, such as:

Ex. 51

If, in this position as the final note on a weak beat, they are followed by a rest, they tend to give an impression of leaving the phrase in the air. This very effect is capitalized sometimes, as in the third section of Lassus' first *Penitential Psalm:*

Ex. 52

The question posed by the text is echoed in the questioning way in which the alto line ends. But this type of procedure is uncommon, and phrases ordinarily end on strong beats either with double whole notes, whole notes, or halves.

4. Common practice in regard to quarter notes is fairly easy to define. The most common situations in which quarters are used are the following:

a. Quicker movement — quarter-note movement — is generally placed on weak beats (beats two or four) rather than on strong ones (beats one or three). Such rhythms as

Ex. 53

are very common.

b. Quick movement on strong beats may be found under certain conditions, such as

Ex. 54

These examples have a quality that is rhythmically carrying because the quick movement is not confined to the strong beats alone, but is linked to similar quick movement on the preceding or following weak beats. Such a rhythm as

Ex. 55

is not common, particularly when the first of the quarters is truly accented. It gives an impression of rhythmical jerkiness or hammering if repeated.

On the other hand, two isolated quarters are less rare on a strong beat of the measure when they are followed by a whole note or a dotted half note. The rhythm becomes stronger when these latter notes are treated as suspensions, since the quarters then tend to lose accent in their presence and to "carry" towards them — that is, to take on the character of being the last notes of the rhythmic group just preceding.

Ex. 56

5. The frequency of use of eighth notes is still more easily described. In the first place, it is common practice to use them very sparingly and always to use two, but never more, in succession. They never appear singly after a dotted quarter, and they invariably come on the second halves of either strong or weak beats.

In the first example the first of the two eighths is a passing tone and continues in the direction in which it started. In the

Ex. 57

second example the first of the two notes is a short auxiliary tone and turns back in the direction from which it came. In the third example the two notes form an ornamentation of the resolution of the dissonant suspension, C.[5]

All notes, with the exception of quarters and eighths, can be dotted whenever necessary or desirable.

Since almost all modern editions of this music contain regularly recurring bar lines, it is common practice to tie notes between measures rather than to dot across bar lines. The notation

Ex. 58

is invariably preferred to

Ex. 59

Quarter notes are tied across bar lines only very exceptionally:

Ex. 60

and the rhythmic figure

Ex. 61

is unusual. It actually reduces the common unit of movement from the half note to the quarter and places the accents where they are indicated in the last example. This causes a sudden

---

[5] This common procedure is described on pp. 80–81.

switch in the pace at which the piece moves and should be avoided by the student in his early work.

If any change in the rate of movement takes place in the course of a composition it is usually in cadences, particularly in final cadences. Here the unit often changes from the half to the whole note, as evidenced by the use of dissonances such as passing tones and suspensions.[6]

The student should be careful never to tie any note to a following note of greater length, since this is foreign to the style. Such figures as

Ex. 62

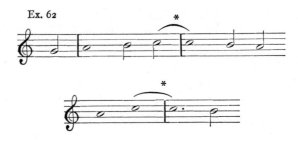

are to be avoided. The rhythmic figure

Ex. 63

is likewise foreign to this style; its similarity to the examples above is obvious.

Rhythm is subtle and very elastically regulated in all this music. The composers were careful to avoid a flat duple or triple meter; they never thought in terms of a dull, thudding, wearisome tread. In secular music there was a marked lightness of step, which can be seen in the works of Claude Le Jeune, Lassus, and other composers of madrigals, chansons, and the like. And in sacred music, where the tone is naturally more

[6] See pp. 71 and 82.

severe, we find not an amorphous shuffling along but a magnificently regulated and infinitely varied rhythm, the imaginative quality of which becomes more evident the more closely we study the music.

MELODIES. *Individual Lines.* The whole subject of melodic movement is inevitably bound up with the problem of rhythm and can hardly be studied apart from it. In the common practice of the Golden Age the same melodic intervals are used as in plainsong: major and minor seconds, major and minor thirds, perfect fourths, perfect fifths, and perfect octaves. All these intervals are used either ascending or descending. The minor sixth is used *only* ascending. *No* chromatic, augmented, or diminished intervals are ever used in the strict style of composition.

There is no such thing as a general direction in which the lines move in this music, as there was in plainsong. Sometimes we find phrases constructed in a manner resembling that in plainsong where the lines flow downwards from a relatively high point to their cadences. When the different lines are at different stages in their descent this produces a magnificent effect, as Ex. 64 shows.

Ex. 64.   Palestrina, *Tribus miraculis*

[handwritten marginal note: This rule frequently broken in Eliz. madrigalists (as pointed out by Fellowes)]

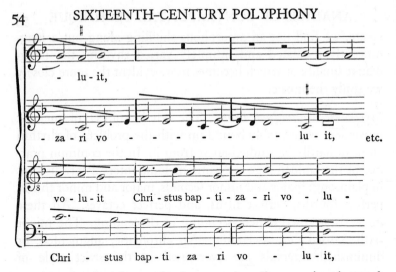

On the other hand, exactly the opposite effect can be observed in Palestrina's five-voice *Stella quam viderant* (Ex. 65), in which the lines flow upwards:

Ex. 65

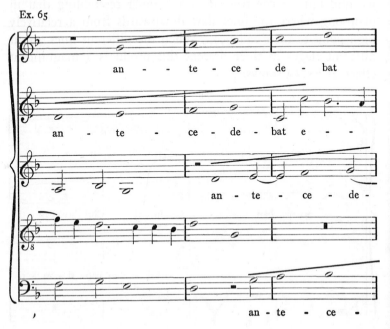

In both cases it is a question of the composer's wishing to echo in the music the thought of the text. These two examples may serve as illustrations of how alive sixteenth-century composers were to certain ideas in their texts and how at times in a modest way they exercised their abilities in painting musically the sense of the words. The student will see, however, that this procedure is very limited and that it is confined to comparatively few pictorial ideas. *(prob. used with more engenuiety & frequency in madrigals than any-where else.)*

Ordinarily the phrases are well balanced in their construction. Take, for example, the soprano part of the fifth section of Lassus' second *Penitential Psalm:*

Ex. 66

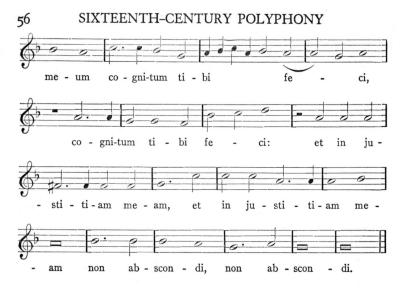

me - um   co - gni-tum ti - bi   fe -   ci,

co - gni-tum ti - bi fe - ci: et in ju -

- sti - ti - am me - am, et in ju - sti - ti - am me -

- am   non ab - scon - di, non ab - scon - di.

The lower limit of the melody is F and the upper limit D — a range of only a sixth. The melody begins on A and revolves around it, going no lower in the first phrase than G and touching C only once. The second phrase with the same text presents only a slight variation from the first, in that C is more emphasized this time. The third phrase begins again on A, touches the lowest note, F, and makes its way up to the highest note, D, where the climax of the melody is reached. From here on, by a successive closing in of both limits, F♯ at the bottom and C at the top are sounded; then begins a kind of final balancing in which B♭ gradually sinks to A and then to G. This melody is a good example of the exquisite balance in construction of phrases which we find constantly in the music of this period. It takes a form like that of a fan opening and closing:

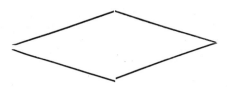

As in plainsong, the individual lines in sixteenth-century counterpoint are never violent. They move predominantly stepwise, and skips are usually introduced for the purpose of relief. Since we are dealing with voices in combination, however, which means that individual lines must not ignore the ensemble, they are bound not to be completely free in the absolute sense. Often we find the bass part in particular moving not so much stepwise as in a manner dictated by the progression of the chords. This happens more often with some composers than with others, and more often in familiar style than in fugal style. Even so, it is remarkable how flowing the lines of the sixteenth-century composers are and how skillful those composers were in manipulating them so that they usually seem to be unhampered by any harmonic considerations.

It is impossible to give any table of rules on how a melody should move intervallically. Such things the student can learn only by careful study of the music itself. Almost the same principles are to be found exemplified here as in plainsong. Stepwise movement predominates, but skips are also a common part of the melodic technique.

The tritone (the augmented fourth between F and B) is an interval which was ordinarily studiously avoided in a line. It was never used in a direct leap

Ex. 67

and it must be carefully handled at *all* times. It does occur commonly in figures like

where at least one of the two notes is sheathed by another note beyond it, so that it gets no emphasis from either a rhythmic or linear standpoint. If both notes are accented by virtue of their length, or by their position as lower and upper limits of figures:

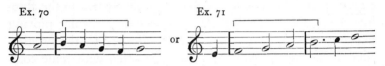

they sound poor.

Individual lines normally tend to cadence on notes in the middle or near the bottom of the range. Rarely does a line sweep upwards to a cadence:

in the way it often does in music of later periods. The student will observe that the lines always stay within a reasonable singing compass (about an octave), and that they rise and fall in their courses but usually begin and end in the most comfortable part of that compass.

Melodic and harmonic sequences are very rare in the music of the late sixteenth century. Lines such as

are practically unknown, though such devices were used earlier and again became common in the seventeenth and eighteenth centuries. At the end of the Kyrie of Josquin des Près' *Missa L'Homme armé, Sexti toni*, there is an interesting passage

(Ex. 74) which is in sequence and which, incidentally, makes use of more dissonances than were ordinarily used by such composers as Palestrina.

Ex. 74

The late sixteenth-century composers rarely cut up music into sequential sections such as these. They preferred to spin their lines out in an ever-varying melodic and rhythmic flow like that illustrated by the melodic line of Lassus' quoted in Ex. 66.

Lines in Combination. There are only three ways in which two voices can move in relation to each other. They can move in similar motion,

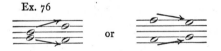

Ex. 75

in contrary motion,

Ex. 76

or in oblique motion,

Ex. 77

All three of these ways are found over and over again, and no one can be said to predominate.

Consecutives When voices move in similar motion there are certain practices which composers take great care to observe. Thirds and sixths are the only consecutive intervals used in two-part compositions, and even they must not be carried on for too great stretches of time, or one ceases to have two contrapuntal melodies and has instead only two voices singing the same melody a third or a sixth apart. Very often we find consecutive thirds and sixths rising or falling in an alternating fashion: *(also frequ*

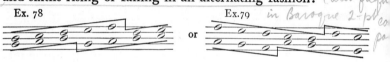

Ex. 78   Ex.79   *in Baroque 2-pt co*
                                                                                        po

but never

Ex. 80

In pieces which have more than two parts, consecutive fourths are allowed, *provided* they do not come between the bass or lowest part and any other. Such movement as

Ex. 81

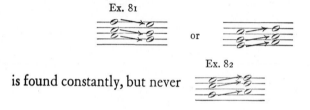

Ex. 82

is found constantly, but never

In other words, consecutive six-four chords are not used, while consecutive sixth chords are common — but again not in too long unbroken chains. *(reflects later harmonic practice)*

Consecutive dissonant intervals — seconds and sevenths — are almost never used under ordinary circumstances.

Consecutive fifths and consecutive octaves never follow each other immediately:

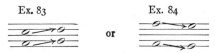

Ex. 83   or   Ex. 84

If they did, the procedure would not be contrapuntal but a mere doubling of the same melody in two parts at particularly open intervals. On the other hand, such figures as

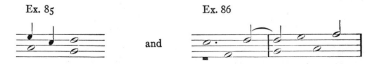

Ex. 85   and   Ex. 86

are common. In the first case the fifths are separated by a consonant note, and the second fifth is actually arrived at by contrary motion; in the second case the harmonic basis changes between the fifths, consonant sixths intervening each time. Figures like

Ex. 87

are not found; the suspension does not relieve the sound of consecutive octaves. On the other hand, the figure

Ex. 88

is to be found occasionally.

In contrary motion consecutive fifths and consecutive octaves

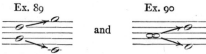

Ex. 89   and   Ex. 90

are frowned upon in scholastic counterpoint. In practice they are rarely used in compositions in only two parts. But in compositions in three, four, or more parts they are often found in isolated cases — not, of course, in sequences.

While it is common practice in contrapuntal compositions for the voices to enter individually at the start, it is invariably the custom to have them all singing at the end and to have them all cadence at the same time. For example:

Ex. 91

or   or

The last chord usually comes on the first beat of the final measure and lasts throughout the measure with no further movement. Once in a while a final resolution of a dissonance occurs in the last measure:

Ex. 92

But in such a case the movement in the resolving voice is very restrained.

6. CROSS RELATIONS. As a result of the point of view that the movement of lines — the horizontal aspect — is the most important, we often find in sixteenth- and seventeenth-century music cross relations which are most charming and beautiful, and yet in no way arbitrary. For instance, in Lassus' second *Penitential Psalm* there is the following passage in section nine:

Ex. 93

etc.

If one studies the alto and tenor lines individually one sees why they flow as they do, even though E♮ in the alto is followed immediately by E♭ in the tenor and then by E♮ once more in the alto. Melodic minor thirds are usually more comfortable to sing than major thirds. In the alto, E♮ comes naturally, being in the signature and making a minor third with the following G. In the tenor, however, the difference between E♮ and E♭ is great. Try singing

Ex. 94

and then

Ex. 95

and it is plain that E♭ is more easily sung than E♮. In fact, after one compares the two versions, E♮ comes to seem farther away from C than it actually is because of the way the line turns.

The music of this period is full of cross relations. The following excerpt from Byrd's *Ave Verum* is typical of the way they are used by the members of the English School, who were particularly fond of them.

Ex. 96

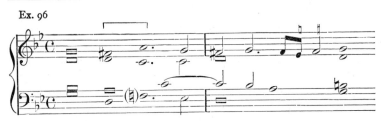

There are no rules for the use of cross relations, except the negative one that they should never be used in excess. Too great a use of them leads to a mannered and even ugly style. One must remember that they are the *result* of melodic movement and not an objective towards which one works.

7. HARMONIES. The actual number of different harmonies used is surprisingly small. In compositions for three parts or more they commonly consist of (1) major and minor triads in root position, (2) major and minor triads in their first inversions, and (3) the diminished triad in first inversion *only*. The diminished triad in root position is not often used, particularly in sacred music. It does enjoy a more frequent use in secular music, but even there it practically always resolves inward to a third:

Ex. 97

Once in a comparatively long while one encounters it in the sacred music of such composers as Palestrina and Lassus. When it is used it invariably comes on a weak beat of the measure and is often the result of a suspension:

Ex. 98

Once in a long while one even encounters the augmented triad in its first inversion. It was particularly effective as used later by such composers as Purcell, but in the following example from Palestrina it is very striking.

Ex. 99. *Missa Quarta:* Final cadence of Christe

In compositions for two parts only, the harmonic intervals used as consonances are (1) the perfect unison, (2) the major or minor third, (3) the perfect fifth, (4) the major or minor sixth, (5) the perfect octave, and (6) any interval greater than any of these by an octave. All other harmonic intervals are dissonances and must be treated as one of the devices discussed in the next section. The perfect and the augmented fourths are always harmonic dissonances in two-part music, but in pieces for more than two parts they are always considered consonances, *provided* they do not come between the lowest-sounding voice

and any other. In other words, they can be used in chords in
root position or in first inversion:

Ex. 100

but not in second inversion:

Ex. 101

except under certain circumstances to be discussed later.

There is no regularity about having a certain number of harmonies per measure. The last measure of a composition always
contains only one harmony — that major triad in root position
which is built on the final. But in other places there may be
two harmonies per measure:

Ex. 102

three harmonies per measure:

Ex. 103

four harmonies per measure:

Ex. 104

or even at times more. Since the unit of rhythm is the half
note, the tendency is away from cluttering the measure with
harmonies, and as the final cadence is approached, the frequency of change is nearly always less. At the beginnings of
pieces as well, harmonies have a tendency not to change often.
It is usually when the piece is well on its way that we find the
rate of change greatest. Such a passage as the following from
Lassus' first *Penitential Psalm* is rare indeed, and here is only
inspired by the words "valde velociter."

Ex. 105

The student will see from the many examples quoted throughout these sections and from his study of the music of the period
how restrained the change of speed of the harmonies usually is.

Without question, all the composers of the sixteenth century
were chord-conscious; but the music, particularly the sacred
music, of a great number of them shows that the chordal aspect
was secondary to the melodic in importance. Chords were not
written for their own sakes; they were rather the result, the
vertical aspect, of the combination of lines moving horizontally.
To emphasize the melodic aspect the composers used a considerable number of devices which created effects of dissonance.
These dissonances, or notes that are foreign to the chordal
harmony, fall into well-defined categories, and will be treated
in the next section.

The student who begins the study of counterpoint must
realize that the spacing of the voices in relation to each other is

very important. Above all, each voice must be kept within its
own range, else the piece becomes impossible of performance.
There are no hard and fast rules for spacing; the main thing for
the student to keep in mind is that the result must *sound* well.
Voices that are spaced too far apart for any length of time produce a thin and often ridiculous sound; voices that stay too
close together tend to get in each other's way and prevent one
another from standing out. This is particularly true when one
writes for men's voices only and keeps all the voices low for a
time; the result is usually muddy. In short, the beginner is
especially advised to begin writing for voices not too closely
spaced.

A passage from Victoria's *O magnum mysterium* illustrates
how effective wide and unusual spacing can be if it is employed
only momentarily.

Ex. 106

The soprano sings high above the other voices for a short phrase.
But in order to avoid the thinness that would result if the

process were carried on for a considerable time the gap is soon closed by the rise of the lower voices and the descent of the soprano.

8. (10)

DISSONANCES. By studying the treatment of dissonances in the music of this period one comes to realize its fundamental purpose and appreciate its importance. Music without it is like food without flavor. And composers like Palestrina, Lassus, Victoria, and Byrd handled it exquisitely. Later, building on the foundations of the sixteenth century, the seventeenth-century composers used dissonance for the expression it gave to music. Men like Monteverdi, Schütz, and Purcell were freer in its use than Palestrina or Lassus and usually wrote music more emotionally complicated than that of their forerunners. No composers have surpassed this trio in magnificence and sheer beauty of expression, and few have equaled them. But it was not the mere freedom with which they used dissonance that makes their music so expressive; it was their knowledge of its basic value and its proper use. Their dissonances are clearly outgrowths of practices in use in the century before them, and they are to be appreciated all the more when one has a knowledge of sixteenth-century dissonance.

In music, as in all works of art, restraint is a basic virtue; magnificent effect is often produced by relatively small means. An excess of any device, or of resources generally, tends to weaken the artistic product, and the greatest artists have almost always exercised a severe selection of means of expression. This can be shown nowhere better than in the treatment of dissonance by the sixteenth-century composers. It was used a great deal, but it was severely regulated.

In a previous section it was pointed out that the ensemble of a composition ordinarily moves in what we should call measures of four beats, a half note to a beat. On each of these beats the basic rule is to use only notes belonging to the harmony.

(In the previous section we saw that the chords ordinarily used are major and minor triads and their first inversions, and the first inversion of the diminished triad.) In order to avoid a continuous progression of mere chords from this limited repertory a considerable number of nonharmonic notes, or dissonances, are employed in a strictly regulated way. They not only relieve an otherwise monotonous chordal progression but also permit the lines to move smoothly.

Two categories of dissonances are generally employed: (1) those which come not on beats, but on the second halves of beats — the passing notes, the auxiliary notes, the dissonances in the changing note groups, and the anticipations, and (2) those which *do* come on certain beats — the cambiatas, the suspensions, and the "consonant fourths." Composers always treat the first and third beats of a measure as accented ones and the second and fourth as unaccented. With one exception — that constituting the changing note group — dissonances are never approached or quitted by skip, but always move stepwise.

Passing Notes. The commonest type of dissonance is the passing note, which never comes on a beat in the measure but always moves on the second half of the beat. It may occur in any voice. It always ascends or descends stepwise from one harmony note to another, regardless of whether the harmony remains the same or changes. It always continues in the direction in which it started.

Ex. 107

Occasionally two may come in succession as eighth notes when the harmony notes of two successive beats lie more than a third apart:

Ex. 108

Although the passing note is ordinarily a quarter note, it is not rare to find it a half note. But if it is a half, it is used only under certain circumstances: it always occurs on the second or fourth (unaccented) beat of the measure — never on a strong beat — and it is nearly always used descending. It often has the effect of psychologically slowing up the rate of movement of a composition, and for this reason is particularly effective in final cadences.

Ex. 109.   Palestrina, *Missa Aeterna Christi munera:* Cadence of the Christe

In earlier times it was also used ascending, and, even though it is comparatively rare, it may be found used thus by Palestrina.

Ex. 110.   Palestrina, *Missa Aeterna Christi munera:* Kyrie I

etc.

Auxiliary Notes. Like the passing note, the auxiliary note never comes on the beat but always on the second half of it. It likewise always moves stepwise, upwards or downwards, but instead of proceeding in the direction in which it started, it turns back to the note which it has just left:

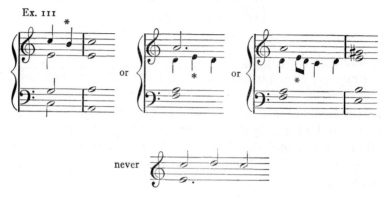

Ex. 111

never

Changing Note Groups. A very common and very effective device used during all this period is the so-called changing note group. It consists of a group of four notes always in the order

Ex. 112

The first note is always harmonic, and may be a quarter note or a dotted half note but is rarely longer than that. The second note is always a quarter and always a dissonance coming on the second half of the beat, never on the beat. The third note is always a consonance, and may be a quarter note or more but never longer than a whole note. The fourth note of the group may be consonant or dissonant, but if it is dissonant it is always treated as a passing note and proceeds to the note a step higher. In the majority of cases, whether it is consonant or dissonant, it moves upwards.

Ex. 113.   Lassus, *Penitential Psalm I*, sec. 3

In the following example the dissonant note in the group is accompanied by a passing note in the bass, with which it forms the interval of a sixth.

Ex. 114.   Palestrina, *O admirabile commercium*

etc.

In Palestrina's motet *Dies sanctificatus* there is a fine passage in which two sets of changing note groups are placed close together just before a Phrygian cadence.

Ex. 115

For extraordinarily fine examples of the continuous use of changing note groups for a considerable length of time the student is advised to examine the ritornello on page 31 of Malipiero's edition of Monteverdi's *Orfeo*, or the last phrase of the first chorus of Schütz's *Resurrection History*.

Cambiatas. Various devices at different times have been called cambiatas. The term *nota cambiata*, which means literally "changed note," has to do in all cases with the exchange of position by two notes, one of which is consonant and the other dissonant. In other words, there are certain times when a dissonance can take the place of a consonance on a beat. For our purposes we shall adopt the use of the term to be found in Padre Martini's analysis of sixteenth-century music.[7] It is a quarter-note dissonance which often comes on the second or fourth beats of the measure, never on the first or third. It comes from the note a major or minor second above and proceeds to the major or minor second below. The note following it must be a consonance, whence the term *cambiata*, or exchange of position. The dissonance always arrives by stepwise movement and proceeds by stepwise movement, and in the Golden Age almost always descends. The following example shows a simple use of the device in the tenor.

Ex. 116.   Palestrina, *Lauda Sion salvatorem*

etc.

Example 117 shows the use of the cambiata in two voices at once, the bass and tenor.

Ex. 117.   Palestrina, *Loquebantur variis languis*

[7] *Saggio fondamentale pratico di contrappunto* (Bologna, 1774), I, xxvi.

In both examples above it will be noticed that the dissonance comes on a weak beat of the measure and is followed immediately by a harmony note on the second half of the same beat.

Suspensions. The sole dissonance which is to be found on the accented parts of the measure — that is, on the first or third beats — is the dissonant suspension. Since it comes at such an important place in the measure it is one of the most important and most effective of all dissonances. Its behavior is always carefully regulated, and there are three steps in its treatment which are always carefully observed: its *preparation*, its *impact*, and its *resolution*. These three steps require the space of time needed for three half notes. The preparation takes place on the first of these three notes, *always* on an unaccented beat of the measure (two or four); the impact takes place on the second of the three notes, *always* on the following accented beat (three or one); and the resolution takes place on the last of the three notes, *always* on the next following unaccented beat (four or two).

1. The preparation is made by means of a consonance or harmony note (it must never be less than a half note in value) coming on a weak beat of the measure. The impact, or dissonant effect, is produced by tying over the prepared note so that it becomes dissonant to the new harmony on the following strong beat. The resolution following on the next weak beat is effected invariably by the descent of the dissonance downwards the distance of a major or minor second so that it becomes consonant with the new harmony.

A suspension can be effected in any voice. The most striking

Ex. 118

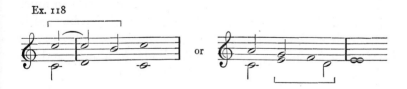

or

ones are those in which the suspended dissonance does not sound
at the same moment that its resolution is sounding in another
voice. This is illustrated by Ex. 118. In the first instance the
suspended C in the upper voice has naturally to resolve to B a
second below, and this B has much more chance of sounding
well and strong if it is not anticipated on the beat of the impact,
as it is here:

Ex. 119

Likewise, the suspended E in the lower voice of Ex. 118
would be much less effective if its resolution were sounded
against it on the third beat:

Ex. 120

A very common exception to this principle is the practice of
sounding the note of resolution against the suspended dissonance if the former is at least the distance of a ninth below
the latter:

Ex. 121

Here the effectiveness of the suspension is not nearly so much
impaired. These are rules which must be strictly observed in
the study of the species; and they are worth remembering, for
too great an infringement of them leads to thinness and un-

pleasantness of sound in the ensemble. They are not invariably observed by the sixteenth-century composers, but they are observed far more frequently than not.

The dissonant intervals for purposes of suspension in the *upper* of two voices vary a great deal in their effectiveness. (1) The strongest and most commonly used of all is the seventh resolving to the sixth, illustrated in Ex. 118. (2) The fourth resolving to the third is only moderately effective in pieces for two voices:

Ex. 122

It is a mild and relatively weak harmonic dissonance which should not be used excessively. When it is used in a setting for three voices or more, however, it can be made more strongly dissonant: *(because in example below creates interval of a*

Ex. 123 *major second.*

Here, on beat one, D in the upper voice forms not only the dissonance of a fourth with A in the middle voice but also the dissonance of a ninth with C in the bass. On beat three, A in the middle voice forms not only a fourth with E in the bass but also a second with B in the upper voice. (3) The dissonant interval of the second resolving to a unison has already been shown to be harsh. On the other hand, the ninth can be used with impunity.

The dissonances which are formed by suspending the *lower* of two voices also vary in effectiveness. (1) The strongest of all is the second resolving to the third, illustrated in Ex. 118. (2) The fourth resolving to the fifth is relatively weak:

Ex. 124

But in three parts or more it likewise can be strengthened:

Ex. 125

(3) The seventh resolving to the octave has already been shown to be relatively poor, since the note of resolution is sounded against the suspended note at too close a distance.

There are three ways in which resolutions of suspensions always take place, and examples from Palestrina's works will illustrate them.

(1) The process of resolution just described is the simplest and probably most usual of all. The preparation, the impact, and the resolution are each made with a half note.

Ex. 126. *In diebus illis*

etc.

In this example there are two different suspensions, one in the alto and the other in the soprano. The preparation of the suspension in the alto consists of a whole note, G, which is tied over to the first beat of the second measure to make a six-four chord, which in this music is always a dissonant chord and must be dealt with as such. The resolution takes place on beat two of the second measure, and at the same time a second suspension is prepared in the soprano on A, is held over to become a dissonance on beat three, and is resolved on beat four. These two examples show the way in which the resolution may take place either a major or a minor second downwards, as the situation demands. The alto resolves to F♮ rather than F♯ because the line is headed downwards, while the soprano resolves to G♯ rather than G♮ because of the cadential formula in which it occurs.

(2) A variation of the process just described is often made by holding the dissonance caused by the impact only a quarter note's length, after which it descends a major or minor second to a quarter note anticipation of the resolution.

resol. with antic.

Ex. 127.   *Benedicta sit sancta Trinitas*

etc.

The first suspension is prepared by F in the usual way on the fourth beat of the first measure. This F is tied over to become dissonant on the next strong beat; but instead of being a half note it is only a quarter and descends to its resolution a quarter note ahead of time. The quarter note E is not the real resolution, however, but only an anticipation of the resolution, which comes as usual on the second beat. This must not confuse the student and lead him to believe that real resolutions can take place on the second half of a beat, for this is so rare as not to form a part of the common practice of this period. The resolution is the same as before except for the quarter-note anticipation. E on beat two is not only the resolution of the suspension just discussed but in this example serves also as the preparation of another suspension to follow immediately. The process is repeated in the same voice on the three last beats of measure two, and still another suspension is prepared on beat four of this measure. At the same time the alto prepares a suspension on this beat which becomes the stronger of the two, for it is a fourth above the lowest voice, while the soprano is a sixth and in reality a consonance. Nevertheless they come down in the same fashion as before, as if both were dissonant.

Once in a while we find the following type of quarter-note movement in the resolution of the suspension.

Ex. 128.   *Missa Quarta:* Gloria

repeat tied note d͡♩.♩ before resol.

etc.

Instead of the dissonance A coming down to G as a quarter-note anticipation of the resolution it repeats itself before descending. The same thing happens just before the resolution of the alto suspension E to D on beat four, and the tenor suspension A to G on beat two in the next measure.

(3) Still another way of varying the resolution is illustrated in the following:

resol. note ⟶ aux. (anticipi)

Ex. 129. *Isti sunt viri sancti*

In this excerpt the chord on F is tied over simply for the purpose of rhythm, not for dissonance. The first measure and the first half of the second are accented thus: ǐ 2 3 1| 2 3 ǐ. The soprano figure C B G A is a changing note group. On the second beat of the second measure the alto prepares G to become a suspension on the following third beat. It remains a dissonance only the value of a quarter note, descends to F♯ as if to anticipate the F♯ resolution, but, instead of remaining there and simply repeating itself, descends to E as an auxiliary note before it returns to F♯. Since the real resolution must be on time on the fourth beat, the anticipation F♯ and its auxiliary E must be eighth notes.

All three of these types of resolutions are very common, and when a series of suspensions is made, rhythmic variation is often obtained by alternating the types.

Ex. 130.   Palestrina, *O rex gloriae*

etc.

An effective device for slowing up the composition, particularly in the final cadence, is the lengthening out of the last
steps of the suspension process, so that whole notes take the
place of half notes.

Ex. 131.   Palestrina, *Lamentation*, Lectio III

In this example all dissonances are treated normally until the
measure before the end. In the first measure the tenor has a
normal suspension, and prepares F for another one in the normal way. In the second measure the resolution is performed in
the most highly ornamented way described above, but with
notes twice their normal value. This amounts to changing the
unit of movement to the whole note instead of the half, and
thereby psychologically making a retard before the last chord.

Anticipations. In this period the anticipation — or *portamento*,
as it is sometimes called — is a descending quarter note which
is usually consonant but may at times be dissonant. It has just
been shown to act often as a forerunner of the resolution of a
dissonant suspension. In such cases it is always a consonance
(unless it anticipates the "consonant fourth") because the resolution of the suspension is consonant.

Less frequently it is a dissonance used in the way in which
it is favored in later periods. Here a change of harmony is implied between one beat and the following. The anticipation
moves downwards stepwise on the second half of the beat from
a consonance on the beat, and remains dissonant for the duration
of a quarter note. When it repeats itself on the next beat the
harmony changes and allows it to be consonant.

Ex. 132. Palestrina, *Missa Virtute magna:* Kyrie II

The upward-moving anticipation is not normally used in this period.

Consonant Fourths. In the sixteenth century the fourth as a harmonic interval was always considered a dissonance when it appeared between any voice and the bass (or lowest-sounding voice). Naturally it could be used like any other dissonance as a passing note, an auxiliary note, a regularly prepared and re-solved suspension, etc. There was one exception to this common interpretation of it as a dissonance, however; it was often used thus, particularly in cadences:

Ex. 133. Palestrina, *Ascendens Christus*

In the penultimate measure the G in the top voice appears on the second beat, making a fourth above the D in the lowest voice, and completing with B in the alto a six-four chord. On beat three of the measure B goes to A in the alto and leaves G a full-fledged dissonance to the dominant harmony. From beat three on, the procedure is regular, and G resolves to F♯ as it would ordinarily do. The only irregular part of the whole thing is the way G is prepared, for it appears on the second beat as if it were a consonance preparing a regular suspension, whereas it is actually a fourth or dissonance above the lowest voice.

Another procedure which is very much like the one just illustrated is the following:

Ex. 134.   Palestrina, *Confitemini Domino*

In this example the tenor sings G on the second beat of the second measure, making a fourth above the lowest voice. And again there is a six-four chord present at the moment. But the alto moves down a second, making the tenor on the third beat an orthodox suspension, which resolves to F♯ on the following weak beat.

The common traits of these two examples are (1) that the fourth is treated as a consonance, since it is used as a preparation on a weak beat for a real dissonant effect on the following strong beat, and (2) that it arrives by stepwise movement. In no case is it ever approached by skip or resolved by other than stepwise movement downwards. The difference between the two examples is that in one case the fourth is approached from the note below it and naturally returns to it, while in the second case it is approached from the note above and proceeds to the note below. These situations, since they practically always involve the presence of the six-four chord, usually come in the cadences, particularly the final cadences. It is interesting to note that this is the only place where the unprepared second inversion of the triad, the six-four chord, is commonly countenanced during the sixteenth century.

Combinations of Dissonances. There are various ways in which different dissonant devices are combined to produce beautiful and effective results in both the ensemble and the individual movement of voices. Often they cause what we would call seventh chords and their inversions.

Ex. 135.   Lassus, *Penitential Psalm, V*, sec. 25

etc.

Here we find in the alto on the fourth beat in the second measure simply a cambiata initiating a new harmony which is not fully realized until the last quarter of the fourth beat after the tenor has moved from D down through the passing note C to B♭.

Ex. 136.   Palestrina, *Sicut servus*, II Pars

etc.

In this example neither of the upper two voices on beat one of the second measure is dissonant with the lowest voice. The two are, however, dissonant with each other; the F in the alto has been regularly prepared as a suspension and must be regularly resolved. But another adjustment must be made after the first beat, for, unless it is, the alto cannot resolve to E without causing the second inversion of a diminished triad. In order to avoid this the tenor moves up a second to C and permits an ordinary triad.

Ex. 137.   Palestrina, *Sicut servus*, II Pars

Here we have on the first beat of the second measure what turns out to be the first inversion of a dominant seventh chord. Incidentally, the prepared Bb is not tied over, but is repeated as an appoggiatura on the strong beat. This is not infrequent when the syllables of the text demand it. The prepared type of appoggiatura is the *only* kind ever met with in this music, and the process of handling it remains precisely the same as in the case of the suspension; the three steps are observed strictly. The tenor has prepared on beat four of the first measure for a dissonance on the next beat. But in order for everything to be consonant when the dissonant Bb resolves, both the soprano and the bass have to move. Whereas the bass is always expected to move a second upwards in these circumstances, the soprano is not so constant, since it has been consonant all along with all the voices, and is therefore free to move wherever it chooses so long as the note to which it moves belongs to the harmony on the beat in question. It can move upwards the interval of a second, as in our illustration, downwards a second:

Ex. 138

or it may skip to another harmony note:

Ex. 139

etc.

The situation shown in Ex. 140 on beat three of the second measure is a very common one.

Ex. 140.   Palestrina, *Missa Aeterna Christi munera:* Kyrie I

etc.

It is interesting because no one voice is dissonant with the bass. The soprano C and tenor D form a seventh which is the only dissonance. The soprano has prepared its dissonance as usual, and it resolves as usual, but, as in the preceding example, when it does resolve it necessitates movement in all the other voices except the tenor, with which it was originally dissonant. It may be stressed here that this particular example is very common and that it practically always acts as it does here.

The following example is a particularly beautiful one, for it moves so well and is so colorful precisely because of its dissonances.

The tenor sings the dissonance in his changing note group at the interval of a third with the passing note, which the alto sings. Then the bass prepares on beat two of the second measure for a strong and beautiful suspension on the following beat. But as in the cases above a certain amount of movement is re-

Ex. 141.   Palestrina, *Adjuro vos, filiae Hierusalem*

quired in other places so that the fourth beat will again be consonant. The alto has to move here, but the middle voice might have remained on C during the fourth beat.

The two following examples of the treatment of dissonance are very common.

Ex. 142.   Palestrina, *Anima mea turbata est*

Lassus, *Penitential Psalm, IV*, sec. 8

They are technically the same, the second containing only more movement than the first. In the first example, G in the soprano is the only dissonance, and, being a suspension on a strong beat, it must resolve to F. E can skip, since it is consonant with everything. In the second example, G in the alto is the only dissonance. It is a suspension whose resolution is quite regular, the most highly ornamented type. E in the soprano is consonant, and instead of moving by skip down to C, as in the first example, it moves through the passing note D. Note that the soprano and alto move in sixths and not in fifths, seconds, or sevenths. If the notes of both the soprano and alto on the second half of the first beat were eliminated, the progression would be precisely the same as in the first example, except for the inversion of the upper two voices.

All these examples reveal how fluid the movement of voices is in this music, and how far the effect of simple triads and their first inversions, which are the basic harmonies used, is offset by the use of dissonant devices. They also serve to show not only how important dissonance is but how carefully and judiciously it is always used.

MODULATION AND CADENCES. It is a rare thing indeed to find real modulation in the modern sense before the end of the sixteenth century. This device belongs rather to the harmonic period when all the modes were subjugated to the major-minor mode — when all pieces began in the tonic and ended in the tonic. When this happened, something in the way of real modulation was logical and necessary if the composer was to avoid a deadly monotony of tonality. He had to be able to pass from key to key in order to sustain interest. The development of the practice of modulation is an interesting one, for even up to the middle of the eighteenth century composers very rarely modulated outside the circle of related keys; it was not until the late eighteenth century that composers began to modulate to more distant ones.

In the sixteenth century, because composers were not tied to the major-minor system, they had a greater freedom of harmonic movement to begin with. A piece did not necessarily have to begin with the same chord on which it ended, and it did not have to adhere rigidly to a tonality. It could move freely, the only requirement being that the harmonies should progress logically and interestingly. This freedom was in force more or less through the seventeenth century and can be seen in the works of such late composers as Schütz and Purcell. Again, arose from the basic point of view that the line gives birth to the harmony, and not vice versa. The only place where the harmonies have any great degree of authority over the lines is in the final cadences, where the bass often moves as it does in later periods.

Ex. 143.   Palestrina, *Missa Aeterna Christe munera:* Kyrie I

In the course of the phrases, however, the lines and their attendant harmonies have a magnificent freedom which is unequaled in the music of the major-minor period. The harmonies do not always move according to the standards of "good" progressions; they do not even pretend to have a preponderance of such progressions as:

Ex. 144

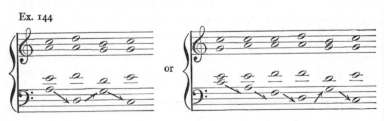

The stepwise type of movement illustrated in Palestrina's motet, *Dies sanctificatus,*

Ex. 145

allows the individual lines to move naturally and flowingly, and the harmonic ensemble (the chords) to progress logically, but not necessarily in a certain key. The effect of the final cadence is sometimes greater than it would be in a tonal composition, for it gathers up the threads which have woven freely moving harmonies in the course of the composition and ties them together on the final of the mode, where they repose. This type of handling of lines is to be found finely illustrated by certain modern composers, some of whom use modern adaptations of the old modes, others of whom make a free adaptation of the major-minor mode.

Modulation in the sixteenth-century sense simply consists of cadencing on various degrees of the mode. This cadencing is not for the purpose of bringing the whole flow of the composition to a standstill, except at the very end of the composition or at the end of a clearly defined section. And, of course, since there is no such thing as a shift of tonality from one key to another, one rarely gets the impression that the center of tonal gravity has actually shifted to the chord on which an intermediate cadence is effected. Usually these intermediate cadences in the ensemble are more or less incidental, and serve the purpose of creating momentary resting places. In fact, they do not occur as often as one might expect, because the dove-tailing of phrases in the individual voices makes it possible to have cadences in these voices as frequently as they are desired, but at different times, so that the flow of the ensemble is not broken.

Final Cadences. In connection with the modes certain types of final cadences were thoroughly established. They are particularly important because they are the goals of the compositions. They consist of the last chords, where all the voices come together in harmonic fashion, regardless of how independently they have moved up to that time. Here, at least, they must all be united, and their harmonic ensemble must sound satisfactory. We may once again mention the fact that in this music there is no real difference between the authentic and the plagal modes so far as the harmonic treatment is concerned.

There are three common types of final cadences to be found. First, there is the cadence which we commonly know today as the *full cadence.* It consists of a progression from a major dominant triad to a major triad built on the final. It is common to all modes except the Phrygian and requires a chromatic raising of the third both in the last chord and in the one which precedes it, in case they are not already major.

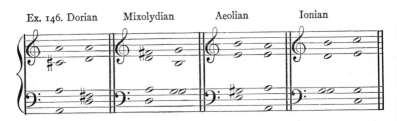

Ex. 146. Dorian   Mixolydian   Aeolian   Ionian

The final chord may be either complete or incomplete. Sometimes we find the third omitted, and sometimes the fifth. In any case both chords are in root position.

Second, the type of cadence found in the Phrygian mode is known as the *Phrygian cadence.* The ordinary full cadence is

never used as a final one in this mode, for the penultimate chord in such a cadence must be major, and D♯ is not available as an accidental for constructing a major triad on the dominant note B. Moreover, the Phrygian cadence is a very distinctive one and sets off this mode from all the others. It consists of the following progression: *= VII̅ (on the Sub-Tonic) → I(♯)*
a modal rather than (tonal) harmonic cadence

Ex. 147

The final chord is again major, although it may sometimes be found with the third or the fifth omitted. The penultimate chord is oftenest found in the first inversion, so that the lowest voice progresses down to the final by a half step. But it may also be in root position, so that the bass rises a whole step to the final. *S. in all these cadences doesn't nec. end on the tonic.*
In any case, the F is never sharped.

c)   Third, an extraordinarily common type is the *plagal cadence*. It consists of a triad — sometimes major, sometimes minor, depending upon the mode — built on the note (our subdominant) a perfect fourth above or a perfect fifth below the final, progressing to a major chord on the final. In the Mixolydian and Ionian modes the subdominant chord is major; in the Dorian, Phrygian, and Aeolian modes it is minor. Both it and the final chord are invariably in root position.

Ex. 148

Mixolydian   Ionian   Dorian   Phrygian   Aeolian

All these cadences may be ornamented with the various types of dissonances which are appropriate to them; the suspension is especially useful in the final cadence because of the braking effect it has upon the flow of the composition. And in order to heighten this retard, composers often make use of the device of lengthening out the steps of the process described in the section dealing with suspensions.[8]

Intermediate Cadences. A student of this music will see clearly that intermediate cadences are generally less frequent and less positively stated than in music of later harmonic periods. This is true of polyphonic music generally; one has only to look at most of the fugues of Bach to observe the same thing. Polyphonic music is essentially flowing in character; compositions tend to move steadily from beginning to end, or at least from one end of a large section to the other. There is no cadencing in dramatic fashion to set off one phrase from another, such as we often find in essentially harmonic music. Consequently, when cadences are formed in the course of the piece they are usually unobtrusive; often the phrases of the individual lines overlap so that the sections are not completely severed one from another.

While this is generally true, intermediate cadences are not rare. Although the voices may not all come to a dead stop, as they inevitably do in final cadences, a sense of cadence is nevertheless evident; and, of course, there are times when all of them actually do cadence together. Pieces in familiar style naturally tend to have more intermediate cadences, or at least more obvious ones, than pieces in more complicated fugal style.

The three types of final cadences just discussed are also found as intermediate cadences, although the plagal cadence is rarely stressed so much here as at the close. The Phrygian cadence is

[8] Page 82.

often used as an <u>intermediate cadence in certain other modes</u> *= imperfect cadence.*
<u>besides the Phrygian.</u> In these cases the final chord is built on
A as well as on E. The first phrase of section four in Lassus'
first *Penitential Psalm* cadences thus:

Ex. 149

etc.

The piece is in the Dorian mode, but this first cadence is
Phrygian, ending on the dominant.

Measures 14 and 15 in the first section of Lassus' seventh
Penitential Psalm illustrate the use of the Phrygian cadence in a
piece which is in the Mixolydian mode:

Ex. 150

etc.

The *half cadence* is likewise important. As in later music, it
consists of ending on the major triad which is built on the dominant of any mode except the Phrygian (where the major third
is not available). The chord before the dominant varies a good
deal, but some of the commonest types of half cadences are the
following:

Ex. 151.   Palestrina, Hymn, *Christe Redemptor*

Dorian

ibid.

etc.

Dorian: dominant of seventh degree

Lassus, *Penitential Psalm, I*, sec. 11

Dorian

Lassus, *Penitential Psalm, I*, sec. 3

Dorian

There is an interesting example of a half cadence which is followed immediately by a plagal cadence in the final measures of Palestrina's four-voice *Lauda Sion*.

Ex. 152

The *interrupted cadence* is one which also has a variety of forms, three of which are very common. (1) The penultimate dominant triad may progress to the triad a second above (our submediant).

Ex. 153.   Palestrina, *Jesus junxit*

In this example the interrupted cadence flows immediately on into a plagal cadence. This type of interruption has remained in common use up to the present day and is very familiar.

(2) The penultimate dominant triad may proceed to the subdominant triad.

This cadence is a bit more unusual in "classical" music, particularly when both chords are in root position. It is less unusual when the dominant proceeds to the subdominant in first inversion.

(3) A cadential situation which is somewhat peculiar to this type of polyphonic music, and one which helps to call attention to the contrapuntal rather than the harmonic aspect of it, is the sudden shift in harmonic direction from the dominant to something quite unexpected. It is met with very little in music of later periods but can be seen not rarely in the music of Bach. A common version of it takes the form of having the bass enter on the subdominant note after a rest.

In this example the most ordinary progression would have been to the C triad. Another progression, hardly more unusual or unexpected, would have been to the minor triad on A. In fact, that is what would have happened here if the bass had not entered on F and destroyed that arrangement.

IMITATION. The sixteenth century did not know the fugue as such, for this form was developed fully only during the seventeenth and eighteenth centuries. In certain respects the classical fugue form is stricter than anything the sixteenth century knew; it adhered to the major-minor mode and made a much greater development of the theme on which it was built. But the sixteenth-century "fugal" style was the forerunner of the fugue, and it has many of the characteristics of the fugue.

The most important of these is imitation. There is no such uniformity as in the exposition of the classical fugue, where subject and answer invariably alternate between the tonic and the dominant, but there are certain notes in the various modes on which the themes begin more frequently than on others. The final is, naturally enough, one of the preferred initial notes in all the modes; and the dominant, or the note a fifth above the final, is practically as important, except in the Phrygian mode, where A is found much more frequently than B. There is no invariable order in which the different initials must enter. Frequently there is an alternation between final and dominant, as in the fugue. For instance, in Palestrina's motet *Dies sanctificatus* in the Mixolydian mode the four voices enter in descending order — soprano, alto, tenor, and bass; and they enter alternately on the dominant and on the final, thus:

Ex. 156. 1. Soprano (Cantus)

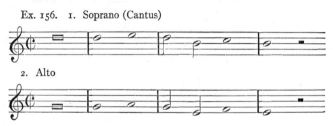

2. Alto

3. Tenor

4. Bass

The motet *Lapidabant Stephanum*, which follows *Dies sanctificatus* in Volume V of Palestrina's works, is in the Mixolydian mode, and the voices enter in the order: alto, tenor, soprano, bass. Only the alto begins on the dominant, the other three voices all entering on the final.

Ex. 157.   1. Alto

2. Tenor

3. Soprano

4. Bass

These details are never constant, but a rough estimate of the initial notes of themes in the various modes, based on an examination of a quantity of music by Palestrina, Lassus, and Victoria, would indicate the following frequency:

Mode	Most Frequent Initials	Less Used
Dorian	D, A	E, F
Phrygian	E, A	C, B
Mixolydian	G, D	C, A
Aeolian	A, E	D, C
Ionian	C, G	F, E

A theme cannot be said to have any required length; and the amount of imitation varies greatly. In *Dies sanctificatus* the theme is three and a half measures long, and the imitation is carried out exactly in the successive voices. In *Lapidabant Stephanum* the imitation is carried out strictly as far as intervals are concerned only through the first five notes; the note values are slightly altered after the first three notes.

An important element in imitation is the amount of time which elapses between the successive entries of the voices. It is rather rare in the sacred music of this time to find entries spaced regularly — that is, to find successive voices entering regularly one or two measures apart. This is flat rhythmically, and the sixteenth century rarely allowed such mechanical devices to recur. In music as in architecture artists were careful to vary their designs so that successive ideas would not appear machine-made.

If a theme in the beginning voice enters on the first beat of the measure (as it usually does), it ordinarily does not begin on the first beat in the next voice, either in the second measure or the third, but in the middle of one of these measures, as in Ex. 158.

Ex. 158.   Palestrina, *Jesus junxit se discipulis*

etc.

Ren. music less mechanical than Baroque music in some ways. (Less strong rhythmically)

In this example there is a wonderful plasticity of rhythm in the way the successive voices enter: the alto on the first beat of measure 1, the soprano on the third beat of measure 3, the tenor on the first beat of measure 6, the bass on the first beat of measure 9, the soprano on the third beat of measure 11, and the alto on the first beat of measure 15. Such irregularity in entries aids tremendously in keeping the rhythm of the composition plastic,

as well as in making each voice individual and not simply a cog
in a wheel.

An example of a short piece built on only one theme is the
Kyrie I of Palestrina's Mass *Aeterna Christi munera* (Ex. 159).
The piece is only thirteen measures long. The tenor enters on

Ex. 159

the first beat and the alto on the third beat of the first measure; the first note of the soprano is halved so that it can enter in the second measure (it could not enter on the third beat on account of the harmony there, and therefore enters on the fourth beat); the bass waits until measure 6 to come in; the soprano enters again at the beginning of measure 8; the alto begins again on the fourth beat of the same measure with a half note; and the tenor enters a second time on the fourth beat exactly a measure later.

Let us make one more observation in regard to the entries of voices in imitation. Under ordinary circumstances an entering voice is more effective if it makes its entry in a register which has been unused by other voices for a time. This is well illustrated by the example, *Jesus junxit*. The first entry of the soprano stands out because the D has not been heard before; the tenor entry stands out because this D has not been heard for over two measures; the bass initial has never been heard up to this point; the next soprano entry is clear, for no voice has sung this note since the soprano herself left off with it a measure and a half before; and the next alto entry is on an A which was only touched a measure before by the soprano. This type of writing is always effective in giving clarity to the individual voices, and for the beginner it offers a valuable principle to follow.

II. **FORMS.** The chief types of composition in sacred music are the Mass and the motet. The texts of the Mass are identical with those used in plainsong, and the number of musical movements is the same. The length and types of writing vary considerably in the different movements of the polyphonic settings on account of the texts. The Kyrie, with its short text, is ordinarily fugal in style and is compactly written; each of the three sections has its own theme and usually forms practically a separate composition. The choral part of the Gloria begins with the words, "Et in terra pax hominibus," after the intonation by the priest of the initial words, "Gloria in excelsis Deo." Since this movement is fairly long textually, the composer usually does not write in an extended fugal style, but rather makes a com-

promise between this and familiar style, in order not to make
the movement too long. The Credo, the choral part of which
begins with "Patrem omnipotentem," is even longer textually
than the Gloria, and very often the composer sets sections of it
in a frankly familiar style. The Sanctus has a short text which
is usually set in fugal style; and the Benedictus, which follows
it, is often set for a smaller number of voices for contrast. The
Agnus Dei is again ordinarily set in fugal style and is broken
up into two parts, the first dealing with the first two phrases
of the text and the second, often for a greater number of voices
than the first, with the third phrase of the text.

The motet, which will be our main consideration, is a variable
part of the Mass. There is no difference musically between so-
called offertories, hymns, and motets proper; the texts used are
innumerable. The settings may be either in fugal or in familiar
style, or an alternation or mixture of the two. Palestrina's four-
voice *O bone Jesu* [9] is a good example of a setting in familiar
style.

Ex. 160

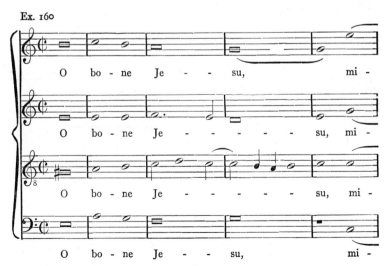

[9] Although this composition serves our purpose here, it is as a matter of fact
probably not by Palestrina but by a contemporary.

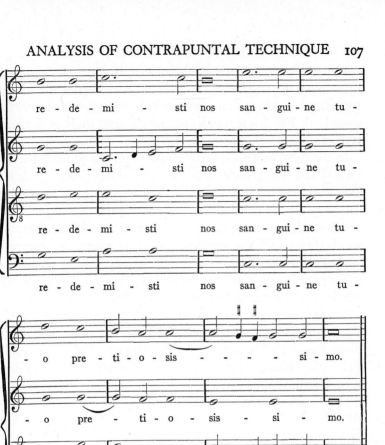

There is no real imitation and no repetition of words. This type of composition varies in length with the text set. If the text is long, the composition will be long; if it is short, the composition will be short, for there is rarely any development of musical ideas in the sense that they are developed in fugal style.

For the beginner in counterpoint it is important to study those types of polyphonic composition which stress the idea of melodic line rather than those which are more harmonically conceived. For this reason let us make a short study of the fugal type of motet.

In the fugal motet the texts are set phrase by phrase. Usually each phrase has its own theme, which is developed more or less like that of the Kyrie in Ex. 159. The composer is usually careful not to allow the developments of the themes of the successive phrases, which are based on phrases of text, to fall apart, but welds them skillfully together, unless, of course, he expressly wishes a distinct break to be made at some point. Obviously, if a complete break were made between sections, the piece as a whole would sound cut up and spasmodic.

Let us take as an example Palestrina's four-voice motet in the Phrygian mode, *Anima mea turbata est* (Ex. 161). The text is divided up into five sections: (1) Anima mea turbata est valde, (2) sed tu Domine, (3) succurre ei, (4) miserere mei, (5) dum veneris in novissimo die.

Ex. 161

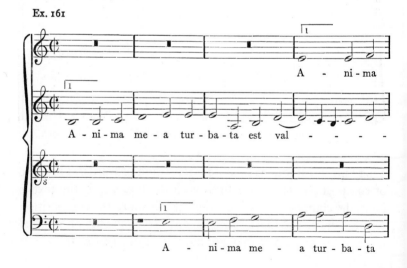

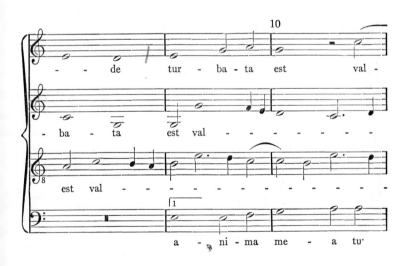

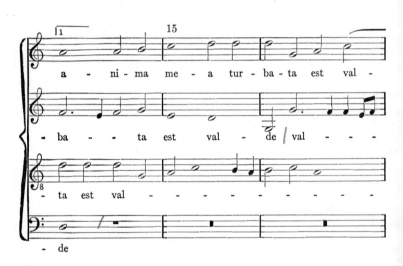

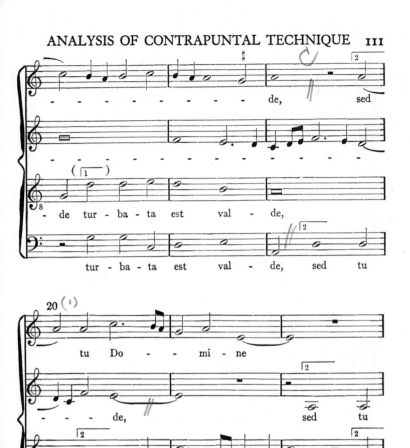

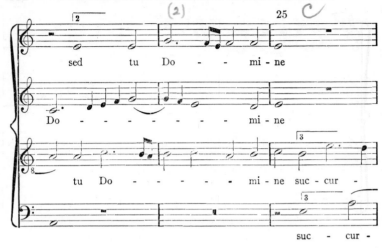

sed   tu   Do – mi - ne

Do – mi - ne

tu   Do – mi - ne   suc - cur –

suc – cur –

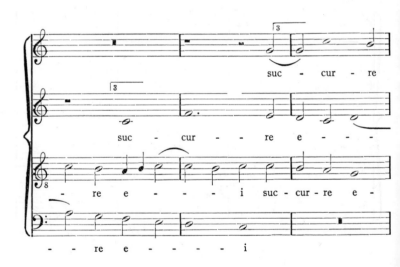

suc – cur - re

suc – cur – re   e –

re   e – i   suc - cur - re   e –

re   e – i

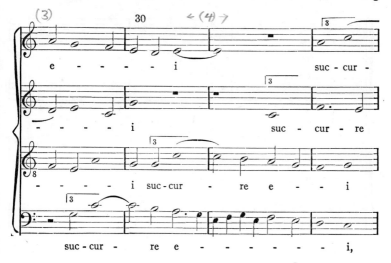

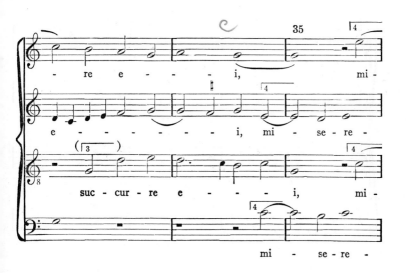

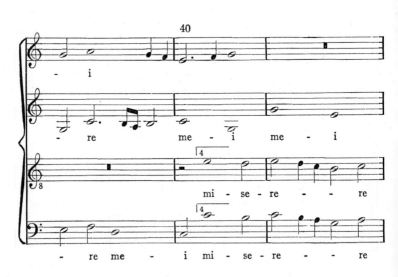

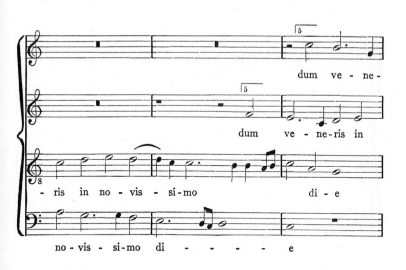

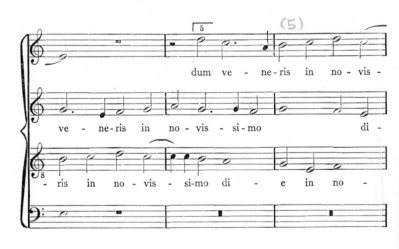

Each of these sections has its own theme, which is developed in fugal style. The first phrase has the theme

Ex. 162

which enters twice in each voice on notes in the following
order: B E E A E D A A.⁸ The section ends at measure nine-
teen with a cadence on A; but there is no distinct stop, for the
bass enters with the theme of the second section before any one
of the other voices has finished its first section. The interweav-
(2) ing of the two sections is worth studying. The second phrase
has the theme

Ex. 163

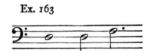

After the first three notes its continuation varies, but those three
constitute a characteristic group which is easily heard when
they appear in the different voices successively. This section,
the shortest of all, constitutes a kind of parenthesis between the
first and third sections. There are only six entries, on the notes
D A A A A E, respectively; and the section closes in measure
twenty-five with a cadence on C. Here again the effect of the
cadence is fleeting, and there is no decided break between it and
what follows.

(3)   Section three is built on the theme

Ex. 164

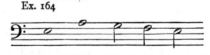

which again varies after these first five notes. There are eight
different entries of the theme, on E B C G G G C A, respectively, and a ninth entry is made in measure thirty-three in the
tenor which does not resemble the others except in its initial

upward leap. The section ends in measure thirty-four with a most fleeting cadence on G.

Because of the text the third and fourth sections are closely related, and this finds an echo in the way the two sections are welded together musically. The theme of the fourth section

Ex. 165

is announced simultaneously by the alto and the bass singing in thirds. There are ten entries altogether, and all but two of them are made in duet fashion in thirds or tenths. This imparts a particularly effective character to the pleading words. The section ends in measure forty-four with a plagal cadence on A — again not emphasized as such a cadence often is at the end.

The final section has the magnificent theme

Ex. 166

which moves mostly in major and gives a brighter and more hopeful character to the end. It enters nine times, on the notes A E F C D A D G D. A very interesting and important thing to note in these entries is the logical relationships of rising and falling fifths between the successive initial notes:

Ex. 167

The motet ends with a plagal cadence, which here is not drawn out as long as it often is.

The composition is technically in no way unusual, although a few devices which are not among the most common might be pointed out:

1. Measure 20. Although D is suspended in the alto it is not a dissonance and so does not have to "resolve," but in this case moves in quarter notes down to C, from which it skips.

2. Measure 24. A suspension in the alto gives rise to a situation like that discussed on page 65. Instead of the chord of resolution on the fourth beat being major, as it usually is, it is here diminished.

3. Measure 29. A combination discussed on page 88.

4. Measures 30–31. The only changing note group in the composition is found here in the bass.

5. Measure 54. The alto has a passing half note descending through the fourth beat. Note that it is dissonant with the acting bass, but that it is treated as a passing note.

6. Measure 59. While the alto and soprano lines are orthodox enough singly, their combination is a bit unusual for Palestrina on account of the sound of the ensemble. They ascend in parallel fourths without a note below to give them the effect of being the upper voices of two ascending sixth chords.

No two motets are ever exactly alike in their structure; different texts call for different settings, and even the same text may be given a variety of settings. Not only this, but different themes have to be handled and developed differently. It is obviously necessary, then, for the student to examine and analyze as many different motets as possible, and to sing them. It is only by this means that he can come to any conclusions of his own as to what the commonest practices are and what departures are made from them.

PART III

APPLICATION OF CONTRAPUNTAL PRACTICE

TWO-PART COUNTERPOINT

HAVING MADE a general survey of the technical practices which are to be found in the music of the late sixteenth century, it remains for us to see how these principles are worked out in music for different numbers of parts and how we may put them into practice for ourselves.

Contrapuntal pieces for two parts naturally lack richness of texture, but what they lack in this respect they make up in clarity and simplicity. They resemble line drawings in that they are complete in themselves. Although they may suggest to the imagination more than the ear actually hears, their chief virtue must consist of the excellence of their lines. These lines must be as nearly perfect as it is possible to make them, and their combination must never sound tentative. The beginning student of counterpoint will be faced with the problem of not allowing his imagination to wander from the two lines with which he is dealing. The more he has studied harmony the greater the problem will be, for such a combination of lines as

Ex. 168

will in all probability not offend his ear, since he supplies in imagination at least one other part and has the aural illusion of a march of harmonies:

Ex. 169

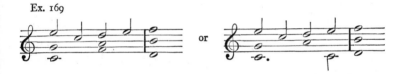

As a matter of fact, in themselves these two lines have nothing inherently offensive in their sound; but in the period with which we are dealing they are never combined in this fashion in two parts only and are consequently not consistent with the style of that period.

The piano student in particular is likely to suffer from these aural illusions. The piano, as I have said, is one of the musical instruments least suited to contrapuntal music. Amateurs and beginners in the study of musical theory sometimes play their work on the piano and make generous use of the pedal, which promptly obliterates the individual lines and makes the music sound harmonic. It is by no means advisable to forego the use of the piano entirely. The instrument is by all odds the most common and accessible one we have and must be used if there is no other way of making the music come to life as sound. But when it is used, at least at this elementary stage of study, there should be no pedal; one should be most careful to hear counterpoint as counterpoint and not just as harmony. One must also be careful not to play the upper part as if it were a solo and the lower part or parts as if they were only accessories to the solo. In truly contrapuntal music there are no prima donnas among the parts. If one part has an outstanding figure in one measure, another part is almost sure to have it soon. And each part must have the assurance that, in the course of the piece as a whole, it is as important as any other part. Almost any fugue of Bach will illustrate this point of view. The best way to give life both to the models and to the pieces we write is, of course, to sing them with other people. In this way each of the lines is brought out clearly, and all are given equal prominence. Furthermore, it is the true way to make the music a part of ourselves.

The student of counterpoint must train himself to hear his first models and his own compositions for what they are: two single strands of melody, each carefully constructed as a line, which, combined, form an ensemble that is satisfactory in sound without any adjuncts supplied by the aid of the imagination.

At the very beginning of two-part writing constant reference must be made to the models in order to acquire a thorough understanding of the common practices in the style. The two-part compositions of Lassus [1] are models as nearly perfect as it is possible to find, because they are consistent and depart remarkably little from the general technical practice of the time. For the beginner this is very important; and for the sake of mental and aural discipline he himself should not deviate from the common practice, which has been analyzed generally in Part II and more specifically in the following pages.

The modes in which he will find his models and in which he should exercise himself in his own writing are the (1) Dorian, (2) Phrygian, (3) Mixolydian, (4) Aeolian, and (5) Ionian.

At the beginning, in order to crystallize as far as possible the flavor of the modes, it is advisable to write without key signatures and to consider the written final as the real final. This will help the student to remember that in this style only the accidentals Bb, Eb, F#, C#, and G# are available. When one has learned to handle these accidentals one may transpose up a fourth or down a fifth, putting Bb in the signature. This will mean automatically that Ab will be available but that G# will be removed from the list of accidentals that may be used.

Diversity and freedom of rhythm are always to be striven for, even from the very first. One of the finest offerings that sixteenth-century music has to make to the modern musician is

[1] Two-part writing is a comparative rarity in the sixteenth century. Palestrina has left practically nothing to guide us here. Indeed, the twenty-four motets which form the beginning of Lassus' *Magnum Opus* (vol. I of his works) are unique as a collection. He wrote them as technical exercises for the musicians in the ducal chapel at Munich, but, like other exercises in the hands of great masters, they exceed their humble purpose. They not only make use of the widest possible variety of technique, but they are extraordinarily beautiful as music. Those students who do not have access to this great collection will find eight examples of two-part writing in the seven *Penitential Psalms* of Lassus. These pieces are shorter as a consequence of being sections of psalms, but they are typical of the technique and are equally beautiful as music.

this. The subject has already been studied in Part II, and in our analysis of the two-part compositions of Lassus we shall see how he handles rhythm in comparatively simple pieces. The problem is one that must *never* be forgotten; it is one of the principal advantages which the study of real music has over the study of the species.

The melodic intervals available are (1) major and minor seconds, (2) major and minor thirds, (3) perfect fourths, (4) perfect fifths, (5) the *ascending* minor sixth, and (6) the perfect octave.

One more thing may be mentioned again here: the unit of movement is the half note, and on each of the four beats in the measure (each beat has the value of a half note) there must be consonant harmonic intervals between the two voices. These intervals are (1) unisons, (2) major and minor thirds, (3) perfect fifths, (4) major and minor sixths, (5) perfect octaves and, within reason, any intervals greater than these by an octave. Two voices alone must never be separated by too great a harmonic interval. If they get much over a twelfth apart they produce a thin ensemble; and they should not proceed even at this distance for more than a very short time before they are brought closer together. No other harmonic intervals than those listed are *ever* used *on* the beats, except in two instances: the suspension on beats one or three and the cambiata on beats two or four. The perfect fourth is very common as a melodic interval, but as a harmonic interval it is always considered a dissonance and is treated like all other dissonances. The beginner must take particular note of this, for in music of later periods it is commonly used in figures such as

Ex. 170

combinations which are never found in our models and should be scrupulously avoided in writing.

Dissonances occur commonly on the second halves of beats only as passing notes and auxiliary notes.

Those dissonances most used as passing tones in pieces for two voices are perfect and augmented fourths, major and minor sevenths, and major and minor ninths.

Ex. 171 etc.

Expanding seconds:

Ex. 172

are common; contracting seconds are much rarer, since their too frequent use produces a muddy effect:

Ex. 173

On the other hand, it is by no means uncommon to find a contracting major second, when the other voice moves away to avoid a unison on the following beat, usually by crossing:

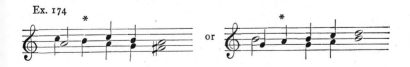

Ex. 174   or

The figure

Ex. 175

in which the contracting major second is followed by a suspension is also very common in final cadences. Dissonances at an interval greater than a ninth are comparatively rare, since there is not much occasion for them if the voices are properly spaced.

Because the auxiliary note is a type of dissonance which always moves stepwise and returns to the note from which it originated, there are certain small peculiarities in regard to it which we must notice. The second is often used when the interval on the beat preceding it is a major or minor third

Ex. 176

and but rarely when the interval is a unison.

Ex. 177

The minor second may come from a minor third:

Ex. 178

the major second from a major or minor third:

Ex. 179

The augmented second is rare, since this style is not chromatic and does not commonly admit it. The perfect fourth can be used either when the interval preceding it is a major or minor third or a perfect fifth:

[handwritten: × 2]
[handwritten: p4]

Ex. 180

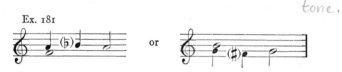

The augmented fourth naturally cannot occur following a minor third; and following a major third it is often altered to a perfect fourth by means of a sharp or a flat: *[handwritten: to avoid the tri-tone.]*

[handwritten: × 4]

Ex. 181

This depends a good deal on the context, and no absolute rule can be said to exist. Finally, the augmented fourth is commonly used following a perfect fifth:

Ex. 182

Both major and minor sevenths and major and minor ninths can be used with more freedom, since the voices are farther apart:

[handwritten: +, −7]
[handwritten: +, −9]

Ex. 183

Cambiata   The cambiata is an effective dissonance in music for two voices. It is never reached or left by skip, and never comes in an ascending line but always in a descending stepwise manner on beats two or four of the measure. Ninths, sevenths, and fourths may be used with equal success when they come in the upper of the two parts:

Ex. 184

In final cadences the major second is often used as a cambiata in the upper voice:

Ex. 185

In his two-part compositions Lassus commonly used only the seventh as a cambiata:

Ex. 186

but other dissonances, particularly the fourth and ninth, might also be used for the purpose:

Ex. 187

The changing note group is rare in compositions for two voices, but is common in those for more than two.

The suspension is a dissonance of common occurrence in *Suspension* two-part compositions. The process of its preparation, impact, and resolution has been thoroughly discussed on pages 75–82, and the student should refer to that discussion once again at this point; suffice it here to say that the three steps in the process must be adhered to strictly, but that the resolution may be ornamented in the several ways that have been discussed.

The almost universal final cadence in pieces of two parts in *Final Cadences* all modes except the Phrygian consists in the rise of the lower voice a half step to the final and the fall of the upper voice a whole step to the final, or vice versa.

Ex. 188

It must be noticed that in the Dorian, Mixolydian, and Aeolian modes this necessitates the raising, by means of an accidental sharp, of the note below the final in whichever of the two parts it occurs, for this note never remains a whole step below the final in the last cadence. In the Ionian mode it lies only a half step below to begin with and consequently does not need to be altered.

The Phrygian mode has a final cadence all its own. To begin with, D♯ is not available, so there is no possibility of the final's being reached by an ascent from the note a half step below it. The Phrygian cadence usually consists of the descent of the

lower voice a half step from F to E and the ascent of the upper
voice a whole step from D to E.

Ex. 189

The process may be reversed, so that the upper voice descends
while the lower voice ascends, but this is not quite so common
and typical:

Ex. 190

The plagal cadence is rather rare at the close of a two-part
composition.

Both the full and the Phrygian types of cadences are often
ornamented in such fashion as this:

*Ornam-
entation
of Cadences .*

Ex. 191

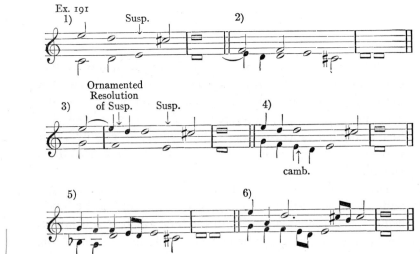

Before the student begins to write complete motets he should familiarize himself thoroughly with the different dissonant devices mentioned above, including the suspension with both its plain and its ornamented resolutions, and he should practice writing correct examples of them himself. When he can do this easily he should practice writing various types of cadences, both of the full cadence type and the Phrygian type, first plain, then with the various types of ornamentation shown above.

When he can handle the different dissonances and can write various types of cadences he may use the beginnings of motets by sixteenth-century composers and continue in the same style. Such beginnings in various modes are given for his convenience at the end of this section.[2] The first motets need not be long, but each successive one may be more fully developed, until the ordinary length of such compositions (from twenty to forty measures) is attained. After he has used enough of the given beginnings to be thoroughly familiar with the various types of melodies common to this music, he may invent his own themes for his pieces. He must be careful to invent themes which are consistent with this style, however, for one which is not consistent with it will be unmanageable as the basis of a piece.

It is to be remembered that the lines must not flow on for too long periods without rests; that they must have direction and an objective; that the rhythms must be varied and not always made to agree with the meter as indicated by the bar line; that the ensemble must sound well; that the spacing must be good; that the cadences must be well prepared; that the whole effect of the composition must not be one of violence but of smooth flow; and finally that the piece must stand or fall as *music to be sung.*

Some of the beginnings given (numbers 1, 2, 3, 5, 6, and 7) make use of imitation, while others (numbers 4, 8, 9, and 10)

[2] See pp. 141–143.

do not. For the sake of practice as much imitation as possible
should be employed, even though it is not carried on for long.

ANALYSIS OF EXAMPLES.

Let us analyze a couple of two-part compositions to see what
can actually be achieved with these small means. They may
serve as models, but the student is strongly advised to analyze
carefully as many more such pieces as he can, for it is only by
familiarity with many that he can determine for himself what
is the common practice involved.

Ex. 192

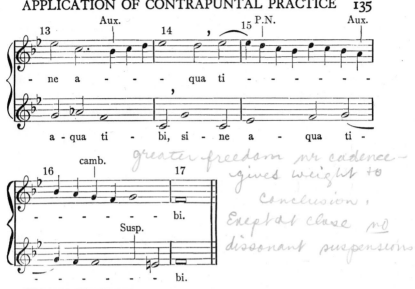

This composition (Ex. 192),[3] seventeen measures long, is in the Mixolydian mode transposed. The soprano and alto each range an octave only, the soprano range (F to F) lying a perfect fifth above that of the alto (B♭ to B♭). It is worth noticing that the soprano starts on C in the middle of its range, touches the upper E♭ in measure 8, and finally reaches the climax F in measure 11, from which it gradually descends in waves to the final. The alto both begins and ends on the final F in the middle of its range and reaches its climax comparatively later than the soprano. In this piece the two voices never cross.

The unit of rhythm is the half note. We find only a part of those dissonances which were discussed in Part II, but they are all used in regular fashion. Only those notes have been analyzed which are dissonances.

The imitation is carried out throughout a good deal of the piece. The alto begins on the final and ends its first phrase on

[3] Section 6 of Lassus' seventh *Penitential Psalm.*

the dominant below. The soprano imitates a fifth above at a
distance of six beats. Beginning the second phrase, the alto
again leads off on the final, and the soprano imitates a fifth
above, but this time two beats sooner, so that it is only four
beats behind the alto. With the word "sicut" the imitation
becomes less strict. The alto again leads, beginning on the
dominant, and the soprano imitates an octave above, its first
note being a whole note instead of a half as it was in the alto.
This is undoubtedly so that the ensemble will not stop on the
first beat of measure 11. The imitation is carried on for five
notes, after which both lines proceed to the final cadence without making any attempt at imitation.

This piece deserves very close study both in regard to each
line and to the combination of the two. The design of line as
such can best be understood if each of the two parts is sung
separately at first. Repeated singing and study in this manner
reveals the perfection of the construction of the lines far more
readily than singing them together. It not only shows clearly the
change in intensity that is secured by the gradual rise of the
soprano line to its climax and its subsequent decline, but also
makes infinitely more apparent the rhythmic freedom which
the line possesses. The same is true of the alto. The soprano,
for example, is constructed mostly in triple meter from measure 7 through measure 14, and it will be apparent that this
arises from the word accents. The feminine ending of the
word "mea" accounts for the feminine endings of the motives
to which this phrase is set, both in the soprano and in the alto.
After this preliminary study of each of the two lines the study
of their ensemble is even more revealing. Their spacing is
handled superbly: each complements the other and yet retains
its own individuality. They never get so far apart that they
sound thin and estranged, and yet they do not get in each
other's way.

The rhythm of the ensemble, as well as of each line by itself, is very interesting. The second voice begins (as is very common) six beats —not four!—after the first. The first phrase seems to move more or less in regular duple meter. But with the phrase "anima mea" the alto picks up its uneven meter 1 2 3 1 2 3 4 which the soprano imitates four beats afterwards, so that the two are singing:

$$\overset{>}{1}\ 2\ 3\ \overset{>}{1}\ 2\ 3\ 4$$
$$\overset{>}{1}\ 2\ 3\ \overset{>}{1}\ 2\ 3\ 4\ (5)\ \overset{>}{1}\ 2\ 3.$$

Even though both the melodies are mostly in triple meter through the middle section, their accents do not fall together to produce a dancelike movement, and the meter of the ensemble remains duple.

The variety of "tonality" which can be secured in the modes is clearly illustrated in the way the subdominant B♭, the dominant C, and even the supertonic G are suggested. There is seldom a feeling of rigid tonality in the sacred music of the sixteenth century, though it is more usually suggested in pieces which are in the Ionian mode than in the others. Ordinarily there is a remarkable feeling of tonal roominess in the modes, and that is one of their great charms.

Another very interesting composition in two parts is Lassus' motet, *Oculus non vidit* (Ex. 193).   *Motet 3.*

Imitation at the 5th (below); 1½ bars after

Ex. 193

O - cu - lus non vi - dit,   nec

O - cu - lus non vi - - -

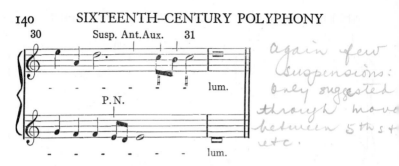

It is not far from twice as long as *Expandi manus* and is in the Dorian mode. Although the piece gives an extraordinary effect of surging, the soprano ranges only an octave and the alto a tenth. The soprano begins on E, the dominant of the dominant, and the alto imitates six beats later on A, the dominant. The imitation is kept up throughout the piece to an extraordinary extent, ceasing characteristically for purposes of cadence: in the second phrase, "nec auris," the alto imitates at the octave below, and again six beats behind the soprano; in the third phrase, "nec in cor," the alto imitates at the seventh below and only two beats behind the soprano; beginning with the word "ascendit," the alto gets still another beat nearer the soprano at a fifth below; in the fourth phrase, "quae . . . ," the alto leads, and the soprano starts out two beats later at the unison, imitating in inversion; in the fifth phrase, "his, qui," the soprano regains the lead by two beats, the alto imitating at the octave below; and the sixth phrase consists of a varied and elongated repetition of the phrase preceding it, the alto leading and the soprano imitating two beats later at the fifth above. How much more varied and more interesting is this procedure than that used by certain nineteenth-century composers in their pieces in canonic style!

In the second phrase, "nec in cor," Lassus seems to have been much more occupied with the rhythms of the notes as such than with giving the stressed syllables to longer notes: "in" gets a longer note than either "nec" or "cor." This type of treatment is not rare in the sixteenth century, even though, for the most part, longer notes *are* normally given to accented syllables. The striking quality of this phrase lies mainly in the clash of rhythms which takes place between the two voices. When one sings the two lines separately the rhythms are revealed to be as interesting and as varied as they were in *Expandi manus*. Again the rhythmic groupings refuse to agree with the meter of the ensemble, although the treatment of dissonance is as strict as before when viewed from the standpoint of the ensemble.

Following are introductory measures of motets which may be used in the early stages of writing. The use of texts is optional.

Ex. 194.   1. Dorian

2. Dorian

3. Phrygian

4. Phrygian

etc.

5. Mixolydian

etc.

6. Mixolydian

etc.

7. Aeolian

etc.

8. Aeolian

etc.

9. Ionian

etc.

10. Ionian

etc.

THREE-PART COUNTERPOINT

THE ACTUAL technique of writing for three voices is not radically different from that of writing for two. It must not be forgotten, however, that the pieces are to be constructed mainly from the contrapuntal point of view; the greater opportunity for richness that is offered should not lead to the neglect of line and varied rhythm among the parts. For the sake of mental discipline, familiar style should not be used too often, and it should occur mostly for the sake of variety in the course of the longer pieces. For specific details of technique which are not peculiar to three-part counterpoint, reference should be made once again to Part II of this book.

The five modes already used are available; the same transpositions and accidentals are to be used when desirable; and the types of melodic intervals remain constant.

Full-fledged major and minor triads in their root positions and first inversions, as well as the diminished triad (in its first inversion *only*), form the repertory of harmonies which can be used on any beat of the measure:

Ex. 195

Rhythmic variety should again be the watchword; this element should *never* be forgotten. It may be useful to emphasize here once more a point that has already been made in regard to momentary cadences in individual voices: lines ordinarily come to rest on a strong beat of the measure.[1]

[1] See pp. 47–48.

Ex. 196

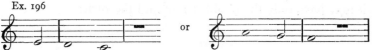

It is rare to stop them on a weak beat

Ex. 197

for this gives a lilting impression not commonly cultivated in the severe sacred style,[2] and the student should avoid the practice. Moreover, it must be remembered that, in comparison with two-part writing, three-part writing usually makes even less use of prolonged quarter-note passages. The greater the number of lines in combination, the more care must be exercised not to let them ruin each other by too much movement. The rhythms of each one can be fully appreciated only if clarity is maintained by means of restraint. Too much quarter-note movement usually results in rhythmic flabbiness and confusion.

The final chord in final cadences, it will be remembered, is always in root position. It may consist only of the root itself in all three voices:

Ex. 198

[2] Once in a while the syllable accents of the text dictate such rhythmic treatment. See Lassus' first *Penitential Psalm*, section 3, where the process is repeated several times. Here the question "usquequo" is emphasized in the different voices by this extraordinary rhythmic effect in the lines.

us - que - quo?

it may have only the doubled root and the fifth:

Ex. 199

it may have only the doubled root and the major third:

Ex. 200

or it may be complete with root, major third, and perfect fifth:

Ex. 201

The chord is always considered to be major whether it has the third or not; if the third is used it must always be chromatically raised in the Dorian, Phrygian, and Aeolian modes. This is not necessary in the Mixolydian and Ionian modes, since the chord is already major.

In the regular full cadence, likewise, the penultimate chord must be major. In the Phrygian cadence it remains of necessity minor. In the plagal cadence it is ordinarily major in the Mixolydian and Ionian modes and minor in the others.

In pieces for three parts, passing notes and auxiliary notes continue to play a great part as dissonances between beats. Moreover, the changing note group is used much more. In this group the second note, which is a dissonance, never falls on a beat but always on the second half of the beat. It may come in any voice.

Ex. 202

or

The cambiata is frequently used and may also come in any voice. Care must be taken to see that it is always approached and left stepwise, that it always comes in a descending line, and that it comes on the second or fourth beats only.

Ex. 203

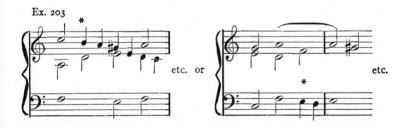

etc. or   etc.

The suspension may be said to gain in effectiveness in music for three voices, particularly in regard to the use of the fourth. That interval, which is comparatively mild when sounded between two voices only, can be greatly strengthened by the addition of other notes.[3] A combination such as that shown in

Ex. 204

and

Ex. 205

is rare in sacred music.[4] In our models such a passage would ordinarily be handled thus:

Ex. 206

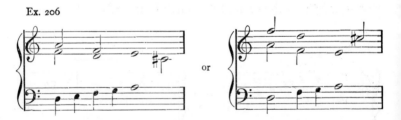

or

Even though the latter two versions lack the color of the first two, they have a greater solidity and were considered more appropriate to the more severe sacred style.

[3] See pp. 77–78.
[4] For a good example of its frequent use in secular music see Monteverdi's madrigal, *Ch'io ami la mia vita*, measure 21.

Again the warning must be made not to sound the note of resolution against the suspended dissonance as a regular thing, except when the former is at least a ninth below the latter. While passages like

Ex. 207

are of common occurrence, such passages as

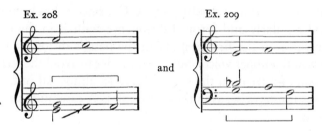

Ex. 208

and

Ex. 209

are to be found rarely in our models and should be avoided by the beginner.

In three parts the "consonant fourth" comes into its own; it is used mostly in cadences, although its occurrence is not limited to this position. It may appear in either of two ways:[5]

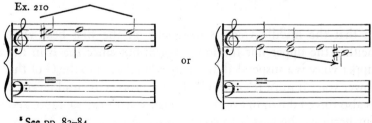

Ex. 210

or

[5] See pp. 83–84.

and it may, of course, resolve with the ordinary ornaments.

Certain combinations of dissonances now will be found very commonly. One of the commonest is the type in which the upper voices are dissonant with each other, though neither is dissonant with the bass:

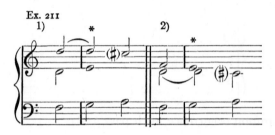

Ex. 211

In these cases D must resolve to C or C♯, since it has been suspended regularly and forms a dissonance with E in the other upper voice on the first beat; G in the bass is dissonant with neither of the upper voices, but it must move to avoid the second inversion of a triad on the second beat. In almost all instances it moves up stepwise, as in these examples. A case quite similar to this is:

Ex. 212

in that the middle voice is dissonant on the first beat with neither the upper nor the lower voice; but since the F in the upper voice is a suspended dissonance in relation to the G of the lower voice it must resolve to E. In this process the middle voice is also forced down to avoid a dissonance with the soprano, and furthermore the bass is forced to move in order to avoid a six-four chord when the two upper voices have moved down. The problem can also be solved by using the six-four chord and subsequently treating the fourth as a "consonant fourth":

Ex. 213

Another method of dealing with the situation resulting from this type of suspension is:

Ex. 214

The resolution of F to E forces the alto down to C, which is treated as a cambiata coming on the second beat and resolving to B on the second half of the beat.

Still another way of treating this combination is:

Ex. 215

Since D is not dissonant with either the soprano or the bass it can leap. If it does this, it almost invariably leaps downwards a third. It will be noticed that there is a remarkable variety of

line and rhythm in these different versions; and when we add
to this the fact that these suspensions can be resolved with the
aid of the anticipation or of the anticipation with an auxiliary
note on the other side of it the variety becomes even more
outstanding.

Let us analyze the three-part *Christe eleison* (Ex. 216) from
Victoria's four-voice *Missa quarti toni*. It is motet-like in construction and will show us how compact a small movement of
this sort can be.

Ex. 216

The Mass itself is in the Phrygian mode, and this movement cadences on the subdominant. It is only twelve measures long, but in the course of those twelve measures the theme is heard in whole or in part thirteen times.

Ex. 217

Yet this theme is used so skillfully from the rhythmic and harmonic standpoints that it is far from being monotonous. Miniature that it is, the piece gives the impression of having considerable length and an almost unbroken flow from beginning to end.

The first syllable of the word "Christe" is sometimes set to a whole note and sometimes to a dotted whole — never more nor less, and it is interesting to notice that though it enters over and over again the entrance occurs at a different place in the measure almost every time. This device has great value in preventing the piece from becoming metrical.

The balance of the three lines as individuals is worthy of note. If one is to get a clear idea of their architecture they should be sung separately as well as together. This brings out the purely linear character and the rhythmic freedom of each line, which may be obscured if one listens always to the ensemble. Notice also how small the melodic skips are in this particular piece, and how greatly stepwise movement predominates because of the line of the theme and the frequency with which it is used.

The bass reaches his climax in measure 9 at the same moment that the soprano reaches the climax of her line. These two voices have been extremely independent of each other up to the end of measure 8, where they join each other in tenths for one measure only and make a fine contrast with the alto, whose entry with the theme in measure 9 lies well not only in her own range but also in relation to the bass and soprano. The climax of the alto comes in measure 10 with the dotted half note F; although the line returns to the same note again in the following measure before it sinks back to the final note, C♯, the accent is different.

The use of accidentals in this composition is very typical of the period. When a figure such as

Ex. 218   Ex. 219

or

appears, the tendency is very often to alter the second note so that it is only a half step away from the first. This practice is by no means invariable; it is only a tendency, and in some cases it is impossible. In the present composition, for instance, the bass cannot enter with E D♯ E as its first three notes, since D♯ is not available. The same is true of the alto entry: A♯ is not available. On the other hand, when the bass enters the second time in measure 2 we find A G♯ A. Likewise in the last bass entry in measure 10 we find D C♯ D. But when the bass enters at the end of measure 8 we find no G♯. This is important because the notes to which the word "eleison" is here set are A B♭ A. The B♭ is such a telling note that it is indispensable as the climax of the line. Try singing the line with B♮, and it becomes obvious at once how important the accidental is here. But G♯ just before it would not sound well, for it would make too chromatic a line and one not in keeping with the style of the piece:

Ex. 220

The cadences are likewise typical. For instance, in measures 4 and 5 we find

Ex. 221

Ex. 222

and in measures 7 and 8 we find

In both cases the bass leaves off on the dominant of the chord immediately following, and the other voices go on alone to finish the cadence. One must notice the effect this produces so far as the lines are concerned. Let us suppose that in the first case the bass moved in this fashion:

Ex. 223

and in the second case thus:

Ex. 224

In both cases the calm and smooth flow of the bass line is destroyed. What is more, the piece becomes infinitely more metrical in its ensemble in these places, and we have simply flat and dull — albeit honorable! — cadences. Harmony, or the chordal aspect, has triumphed and has forced the individual lines to obey it. In fugal style, however, the sixteenth century did not permit its lines to be dictated to in any such absolute fashion, even though it by no means despised the harmonic aspect of music; indeed, it regulated harmonies and dissonances very carefully, as we have already had ample occasion to observe.

As mentioned above, the piece ends on the subdominant, for it is to be followed immediately by the final Kyrie which cadences on the final. If it had not stood between the two Kyries it might just as well have cadenced thus:

Ex. 225

All the dissonances are typical and have already been described in Part II. Let us look, however, at the treatment of the fourth as a harmonic interval, since it appears for the first time in music for three voices. In measure 4 on beats two, three, and four there is in the alto a fourth prepared and resolved like any other dissonant suspension, and, as so often happens, it involves the presence of a six-four chord. In measure 6 there is in the soprano a regularly prepared and resolved fourth without an accompanying sixth. At the juncture of measures 7 and 8 we find in the soprano an example of the "consonant fourth" — so-called because its preparation was not made as a real consonance.

Let us now examine a composition which is in the Aeolian mode and which is composed of two sections, each having its own theme:

Ex. 226. Palestrina, "Pleni sunt coeli," from *Missa Gabriel Archangelus*

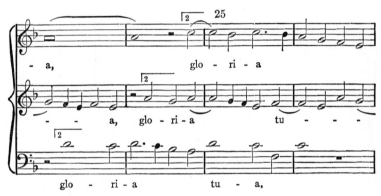

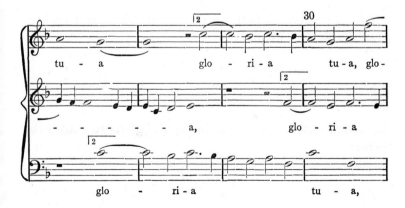

The first section is built on the words "pleni sunt coeli et terra" and has the theme:

Ex. 227

the second section is built on the words "gloria tua" with the theme:

Ex. 228

A variation of theme II occurs twice in the form

Ex. 229

and accompanies the original two beats after its entry. The two sections are about equal in length. The first has eight well-defined entries of the theme, while the second has twelve well-defined entries (counting two entries of the variation). Besides the twelve in the second part there are several others which are worth noting. In measure 21 the alto enters with a theme that is really theme II with the interval between the second and third notes altered; in measure 30 the soprano enters on the fourth beat with theme II without its first two notes; in measures 34 and 35 there is an overlapping of theme II and its variation, as in measures 17 and 18.

The whole composition is remarkable on account of its smooth flow and its lack of bald cadences where all the voices stop dead together. And yet it is full of air — each voice has plenty of rests throughout, or places in the line where breath may be taken.

Structurally one of the most interesting places is the connection between the two sections. The bass has a beautiful cadence in measures 16 and 17, the alto another two beats later. The remarkable aspect of measure 17, however, is the way the soprano keeps the first section from coming to a stop before the second section begins. She does it by means of the beautiful long line which in main outline in measures 16, 17, and 18 is

Ex. 230

and does not permit the use of C♯, the leading tone. Thus the

flow continues unbroken. In fact, there is more than a sugges-
tion of the variation of theme II in the soprano part beginning
at the middle of measure 15, which runs into an actual statement of theme II beginning on the last beat of measure 16.

In this composition the way the lines behave in regard to each
other is worth noticing, because it is so typical of the period.
For instance, the crossing back and forth between the soprano
and the alto in measures 21 and 22 and in measures 26 and 27
not only results in long lines which flow smoothly but also
gives a remarkable play of voice color. The tone quality of the
soprano and alto voices is different by nature, and in such
passages as those just cited the two voices have particular charm
and beauty, for neither loses its individuality in the process of
weaving; now the lighter tone quality is on top, now under-
neath, now again on top. Played on the piano, such a passage
is merely stupid, since there is no difference in tone color, but
with two orchestral instruments of different tone colors the
same differentiation becomes apparent as with voices. The effect
is magnificently exploited by Bach in such pieces as the trio-
sonatas for organ, where each line must be played on a separate
keyboard. While this device of crossing voices for the sake of
tone color is by no means rare in sacred music of the sixteenth
century, it is in secular music of the period that it is used most
often; there it really flowers.

The dissonances in *Pleni sunt coeli* are all most orthodox.
Measure 25 contains an interesting treatment of dissonance consisting of a suspension resolving regularly at the same time that
a cambiata is used in the alto.

When the student has examined enough pieces for three
voices so that he feels familiar with the technique, he should
begin as he did when writing for two voices. First he should
gain facility in writing examples of all the different kinds of
dissonances in each of the three voices; then he should write

cadences of different kinds. These technical details should be thoroughly mastered before he begins the construction of phrases with imitations.

As beginnings of his first motets he may use those given below. Various beginnings set different problems. Number 1 has nothing unusual about it, for the bass begins on the dominant, the tenor answers on the final, and the alto enters on the dominant. Number 2 begins in almost the opposite fashion, the alto entering on the subdominant instead of the dominant. Number 3 varies slightly in that the subject begins in the tenor on the fourth degree of the mode (as it often does in the Phrygian) and the bass answers on the final. Number 10 presents an interesting problem in that the alto enters with the theme inverted after the first interval.

Ex. 231. 1. Dorian

2. Dorian

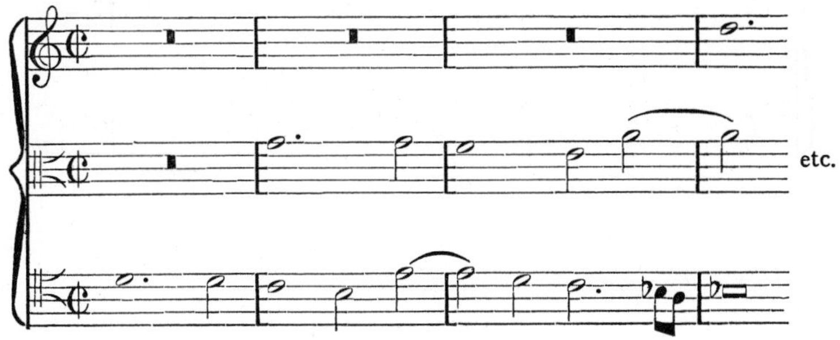

3. Phrygian

etc.

4. Phrygian

etc.

5. Mixolydian

etc.

6. Mixolydian

7. Aeolian

8. Aeolian

9. Ionian

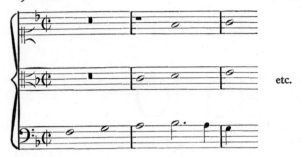

etc.

10. Ionian

etc.

FOUR-PART COUNTERPOINT

THE STUDENT will find that the progression from three- to four-part writing again involves nothing positively new. The difficulty which is added is simply that of handling a fourth voice and making necessary adjustments in the ensemble so that, while each one maintains as much individuality as possible, all the voices sound quite at home with each other. With the still greater opportunity for richness of ensemble, the student must be on his guard not to allow his lines to become metrical and not to permit any one to usurp too much melodic importance at the expense of the others. He must watch his bass part particularly to see that it does not become merely a harmonic bass but that it retains real melodic interest the same as any of the other voices.

By this time he should be so well acquainted with the style with which he is dealing that a rehearsal of the elementary points is unnecessary. Needless to say, the five modes are still to be used; the same melodic intervals hold; no additions are to be made to the repertory of harmonies available; and the same dissonances are at his disposal as before.

Variety of rhythm, which is the very core of good counterpoint, should be cultivated relentlessly. No student should be satisfied with permitting his four voices to progress for long periods in the same rhythms, unless he does so purposely for the sake of setting off passages in familiar style against fugal sections. The latter procedure is very common — and very effective. But it is not the same as allowing oneself to slip into a harmonic style by accident, through forgetfulness of the rhythmic independence of the lines.

There should be no relaxation of technique, since one of the greatest values in adhering to such a strict style is the discipline involved.

Compositions for four parts are ordinarily of greater length than those for two or three, especially when fugal treatment is used most of the time. While pieces in two or even three parts are necessarily limited in length on account of the relative sparsity of means, those for four or more parts are often developed in an architectural fashion until they consist of a hundred measures or more. This is made possible by the fact that four voices or more offer much greater opportunity for variety in color effect and for the passing of themes back and forth in a way to impress the emotional idea of the text upon the listener. In comparison with pieces for four parts, those for two or three parts often seem like miniatures. It is in the longer pieces that the student gets real experience in building: in keeping the composition going properly by dovetailing sections, but at the same time making sure that the music has air and does not plod along monotonously and drearily for great stretches of time. Anyone will recognize that the same problems of construction are present here as in a literary essay. Too much repetition makes for monotony; on the other hand, ideas must proceed in an orderly fashion, so that they are not wasted but are given proper expression and emphasis.

Voices may enter in whatever order is most effective: soprano, alto, tenor, bass; bass, alto, tenor, soprano; bass, tenor, alto, soprano; alto, tenor, bass, soprano; and so on. It will be noticed, moreover, that the order used at the beginning is by no means always retained as the piece progresses; on the contrary, it is very apt to change, and to change frequently, so that any voice may lead off with a theme regardless of whether it has done so in previous sections or not. This matter of successive entries has already been treated in Part II in the section dealing with imitation, which may be referred to also for a discussion of the length of time which elapses between successive entries.

The most satisfactory way of seeing how the process of construction is managed is to study good models in detail. Naturally, no two motets are constructed exactly alike any more than any two fugues or any two movements in sonata form are. They have in common certain well-defined characteristics, but the working out of architectural details must be handled in somewhat different fashion in each composition.

Let us look, for example, at Palestrina's four-part *In diebus illis* (Ex. 232), which is fugal throughout. Unlike many motets, it makes no use whatever of familiar style as such, so that contrast and interest are maintained without recourse to setting off harmonic sections against contrapuntal ones. Before any attempt is made to look into the technical features of this piece, however, the student should become well acquainted with it through singing. He should know very well how it *sounds*, not only from the standpoint of ensemble but also from the standpoint of the individual lines.

Ex. 232

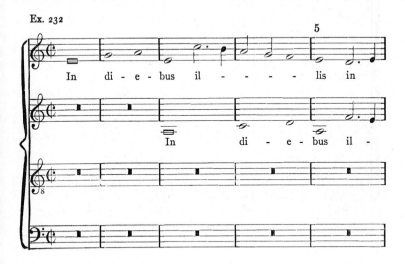

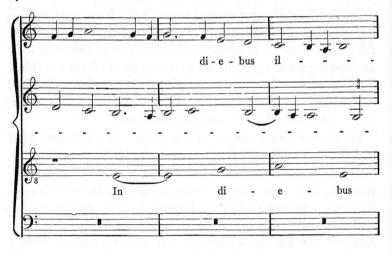

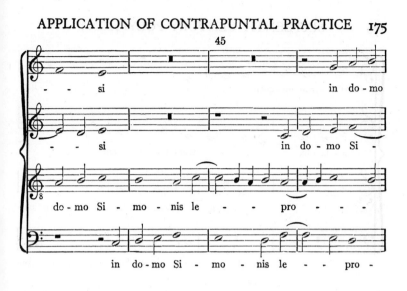

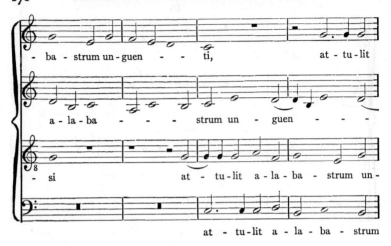

- ba - strum un - guen - - ti,   at - tu - lit

a - la - ba - - - strum un - guen - - -

- si   at - tu - lit a - la - ba - strum un -

at - tu - lit a - la - ba - strum

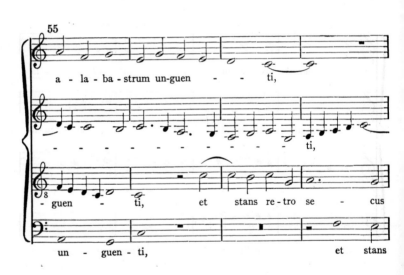

a - la - ba - strum un-guen - - ti,

- - - - - - - - - - ti,

- guen - ti,   et stans re - tro se - cus

un - guen - ti,   et stans

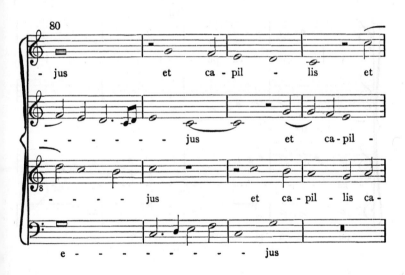

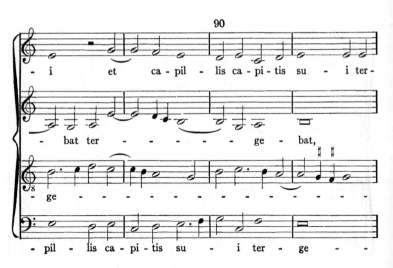

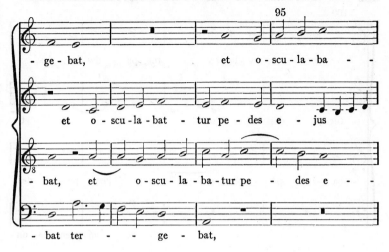

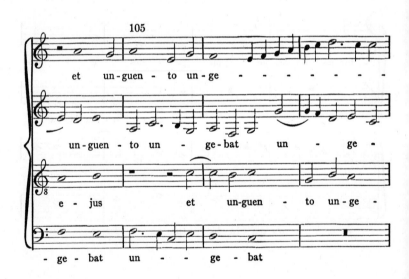

At first sight this composition seems to be somewhat monotonous, but the more one studies its construction the more remarkable it appears. There are surprisingly few cadences which
produce a real impression of stopping. The sections are so skillfully dovetailed that the flow of music is never really interrupted

from beginning to end; yet there are numerous resting places for the individual voices. One cannot insist enough upon careful study of the manner in which each of these lines begins after resting and cadences before resting; the phrasing of each line is completely characteristic of the reposeful and serene nature of the music.

The piece, which is in the Aeolian mode, balances between A and C as centers of tonality. A is naturally predominant: it not only prevails at the beginning and at the end but figures throughout the piece, and C as a center appears only at intervals to relieve it. For example, from measures 16 to 25 C is prominent and is only prevented from becoming dominant over A by the cadence in measures 25 and 26. Again, about measure 43 C begins to assume an importance which grows steadily until it is curbed about measure 70. And in measures 77 and 78 it succeeds in wresting enough attention from A to demand a very definite cadence. After this cadence it is distinctly uppermost until measure 91, when the balance shifts so that A gradually wins the upper hand and brings the piece to a close. But throughout there is no violence in this kind of contest for superiority; the problem of balancing these two centers, with A always a little heavier than C, is handled by Palestrina with the most exquisite delicacy. This system is entirely different from the one in force during the eighteenth and early nineteenth centuries, when tonality was much more settled, when one key at a time was dominant, and when a frank and distinctly audible shift — modulation in the present-day sense — was necessary in order to go from the established key to a new key, which in its turn became established. There are all shades of variation between these clearly defined procedures. Even in Purcell, who is usually fairly close to the major-minor system of tonality, there is very often a peculiarly swift shifting back and forth from one key to another which is more than reminiscent of the balancing system in the century before him. The

same thing may be said of a great deal of modern music. In his
mature works Fauré is particularly fond of this delicate balancing of tonal centers. The moderns, however, restrict themselves
much less in their choice of centers than the early composers
with whom we are dealing, and they do not hesitate to go much
farther afield. The whole problem is a very important one for
the student of music, and one to which he should give much
thought, particularly once he has acquired a certain proficiency
in the more elementary details. The longer his compositions the
more important it becomes if he is to achieve the consistency and
avoid the monotony that were mentioned earlier in this chapter.

The text of this motet deals with the familiar story of the
women who anointed and washed and kissed the feet of Jesus
as he sat at table in the house of Simon the leper. It is treated in
the typical motet fashion: each phrase has its own theme, which
is more or less strict, depending on the circumstances. Entries
are actually made on every degree of the mode, but it is to be
noted that A, G, E, and C are by far the most frequent as initial
notes of a phrase. A is most frequent of all, and E as a fifth
above it is often used to alternate with it in a section, D being
so used once in a while; G likewise is a frequent initial, and
usually alternates with C, the fifth below. Now it is a significant
fact that it is in precisely those measures where the tonal balance
most inclines to C that these two initials, G and C, have their
greatest frequency. F is used comparatively rarely, and then it
alternates mostly with C (beginning in measure 56), while B is
used only once in the whole piece — in the soprano in measure
32 — and is answered in the alto immediately by E a fifth
below. Entries in any one section, then, tend to be made fairly
constantly at the intervals of a fifth above or below or of a fourth
above or below:

Ex. 233

with a slight tendency at comparatively rare times towards such intervals as

Ex. 234

Palestrina's motet *Dies sanctificatus* [1] in the Mixolydian mode is a good illustration of the alternation of fugal style with familiar style.

Ex. 235

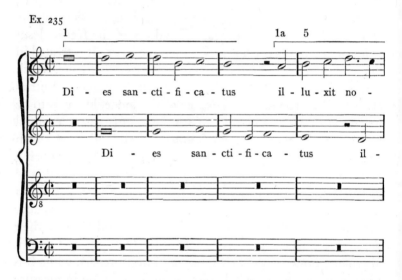

[1] This motet has been used many times as an illustration. It is chosen again here because it is such a good example of Palestrina's technique in setting off fugal style against familiar style. A good analysis of it may be found in Jeppesen's *Kontrapunkt*.

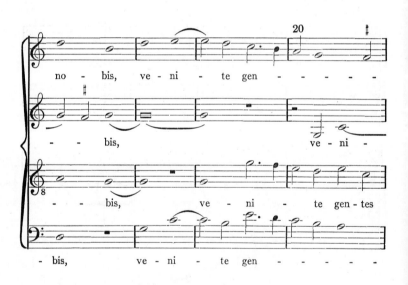

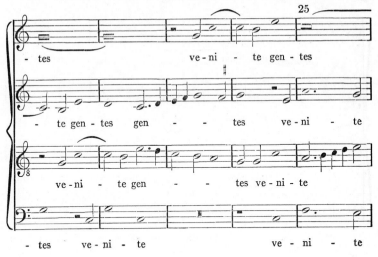

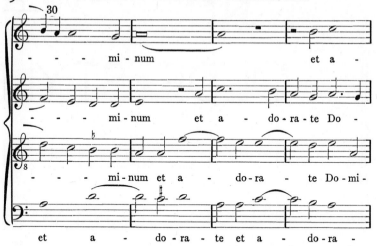

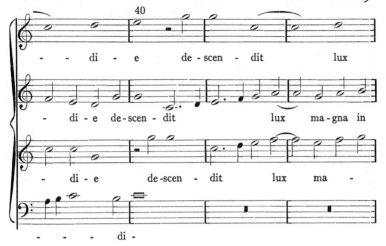

SIXTEENTH–CENTURY POLYPHONY

50

de - scen - dit lux ma -

- dit lux ma - gna in ter - ris;

lux ma - gna in ter - ris lux ma - gna in

- scen - dit lux ma - gna in ter -

- gna in ter - ris; haec di - es quam

haec di - es quam fe - cit

ter - - ris; haec di - es

- - - ris; haec di - es

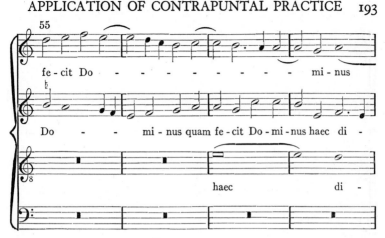

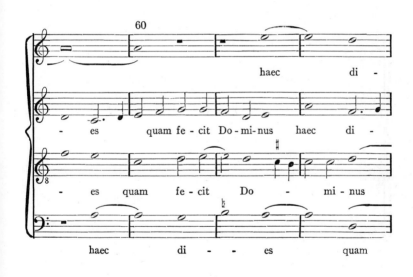

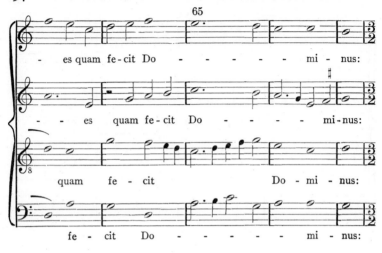

- es quam fe - cit Do - - - - - mi - nus:

- - es quam fe - cit Do - - - - mi - nus:

quam fe - cit Do - mi - nus:

fe - cit Do - - - - mi - nus:

Ex - ul - te - mus et lae - te - mur in e -

Ex - ul - te - mus et lae - te - mur in e -

Ex - ul - te - mus et lae - te - mur in e - a

Ex - ul - te - mus

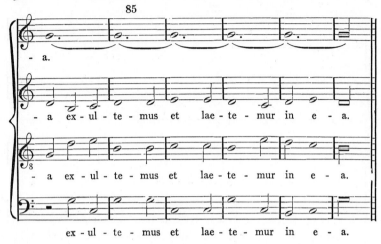

With the exception of the three measures beginning with measure 37 and the concluding section, beginning with measure 68, the piece is treated fugally. The theme of the first section consists of two elements, 1 and 1a, which are first introduced only by the soprano and alto parts in duet fashion. In measure 8 the tenor and the bass enter, imitating the soprano and the alto exactly up to measure 15. But their entries are timed differently, for the tenor and bass begin on beat three of their respective measures, whereas the soprano and the alto begin on beat one. The entries of the soprano and alto in measure 10 are made with new bits of melodic material so that they will not detract from the duet character of the tenor and bass even though they continue along with the lower voices.

The second section is not treated too strictly in the matter of imitation, although the melody of the bass beginning in measure 18 is more or less the norm, with two upward skips of a fourth separated by a descending second. Moreover, the melody of "et adorate," resembles closely that of "venite"; here the imitation is often free, the main characteristic of the theme being a

rise from the first note to the second, followed by a scalewise
descent. Although the motet begins in a joyful and rather
exuberant tone, it begins to grow calmer in the "venite" section
because of the falling lines. In the "et adorate" section this impression of growing calm is increased by the introduction of
changing note groups in the different voices and by the elimina-
tion of the second leap of a fourth upwards in the theme. Palestrina, of course, already has his eye on the word "descendit,"
for which he wishes to make the greatest effect possible; in
order to let it break through and shine he prepares it by the
unusual calm of which we have been speaking. The very short
passage in familiar style which forms the setting of "quia
hodie" gives the impression of having practically no motion at
all. It is preceded by an extraordinarily beautiful Phrygian
cadence, and its very long notes result in a kind of suspended
animation — a stillness, yet a tension, which presages an out-
break. It serves to set off to unusual advantage the following
fugal section dealing with "descendit." The sixteenth-century
composer must have rejoiced at setting such a word as "descendit" to music, for he usually makes a downward leap in the
melody. When this leap is passed from one voice to another as
it is here (and this is typical) the effect is very striking and im-
pressive, particularly when the voices enter in such quick
succession.

Such modest bits of dramatic expression are not uncommon
in the sixteenth century, but they are never obtrusive, for sacred
music of this period was never meant to call too much attention
to itself. At the same time, the method used here by Palestrina
is basically the same as the one which Beethoven used constantly
more than two centuries later, and which can be seen, for example, in the first movement of his D major piano sonata from
opus 10: toward the end of the exposition and again near the
end of the movement a theme in half notes is set off dramatically
from the preceding eighth-note movement, so that it tends to

store up energy for the subsequent plunge into quarter and then eighth notes again. It is in the spirit more than in the letter that Palestrina here predicts Beethoven, of course; but the sixteenth-century composer is by no means the dull and expressionless writer which those who are not really acquainted with this music often accuse him of being. The subtlety of his writing is lost on such people; he does not pretend to astonish the jaded modern ear. But for those who are willing to study and listen there is a vast treasure of expressiveness in his music.

Beginning with the "descendit" section the piece resumes its joyful character. "Haec dies" is calmer in tone and is enriched enormously from measure 53 on by the introduction of B♭, which swings the tonal balance toward the minor dominant. This balance is partly restored by the cadence on the final but not completely, because the cadence is only a type of half cadence which serves to introduce the final "exultemus" section.

The triple-measure concluding section is in a modified familiar or chordal style. The practice of ending a motet in triple time is by no means uncommon if the text permits — that is, if the final word of it is "alleluia," or if it is of a joyous nature, as in the present instance. Although the section is all in triple time it does not plod along in regularly recurring rhythms from beginning to end. The first three measures are trochaic in all the voices. The soprano continues with a combination of trochee and iambus; the alto with a combination of iambus and trochee; and the tenor with a combination of tribrach and iambus. In the sixth measure of the section the tenor makes a start with the theme which the soprano sang in the first measure, and in the eighth the soprano starts with the theme the alto sang in the first. After the cadence on C in measure 78 the soprano takes up the original alto theme in earnest, while the tenor sings the original soprano theme, and the bass combines the first two measures of his own theme with that of the original tenor. The piece is brought to a close by a joyous plagal cadence so extended that the alto and tenor have a chance to cross and recross while the soprano holds to the final and the bass is treated in true bass fashion, skipping back and forth from the final to the subdominant.

The treatment of dissonance in this final section is worth noting. On the whole, it plays very little part. Only the suspension is used. Its use can best be seen if we bar the first five measures thus:

Ex. 236

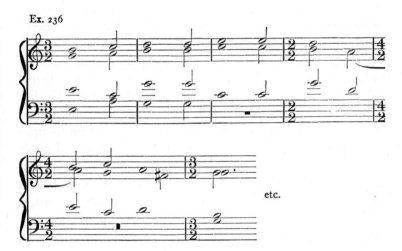

etc.

This is exactly the aural effect, since the impact of the dissonance in the suspension process always creates accent. Such treatment results in a striking and at the same time delightful upset in the meter and prevents its becoming too regularly triple in character. This is another illustration of the sixteenth-century composer's dislike for monotony of rhythm and his richness in means of varying it. We must never forget this indispensable element, variety of rhythm, in good counterpoint.

The student may follow the same procedure in beginning his study of four-part counterpoint as he did in two- and three-part writing: he should first practice using different dissonances in each of the four lines, then write different cadences, and finally use the beginnings of motets in the different modes given below. He should examine and analyze as much music as possible, using Part II as a guide for such study.

Although in the course of his analyses he will occasionally find devices not included in the common practice as outlined in this book, he should forego their use until he is absolutely sure of his technique within the common practice. The English School departs most from what is outlined here; the sacred music of such composers as Tallis and Byrd contains innumerable practices peculiar to it alone, particularly in regard to cadence formulae. When one is thoroughly familiar with the *common* practice of the time, these differences in the English School tend to stand out all the more and to give English music its distinguishing stamp. These departures from common practice are made, to a lesser degree perhaps, in most sacred music by composers other than Palestrina, Lassus, and Victoria. The main reason for adhering so rigidly to the common practice is to acquire discipline, without which no progress can be made, and a basic appreciation of contrapuntal technique that may serve not only as a springboard for further technical analysis of both earlier and later music but also as a basis for composition itself.

The following are optional beginnings of four-part motets for use at the start of four-part writing.

Ex. 237. 1. Dorian

2. Dorian

3. Phrygian

etc.

4. Phrygian

etc.

5. Mixolydian

etc.

6. Mixolydian

etc.

7. Aeolian

etc.

8. Aeolian

etc.

9. Ionian

etc.

10. Ionian

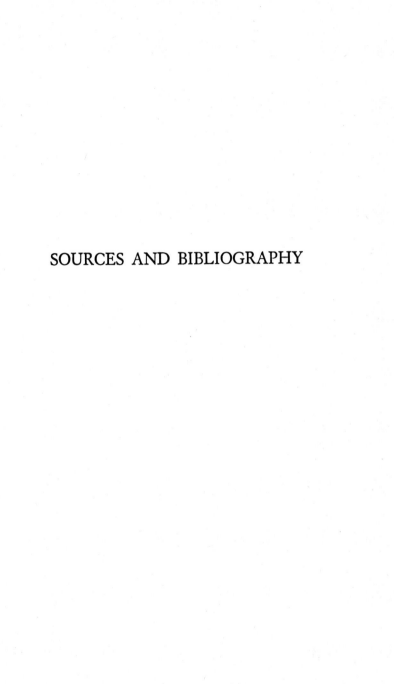

SOURCES AND BIBLIOGRAPHY

SOURCES OF ILLUSTRATIONS

BIBLIOGRAPHY

I. BOOKS ON PLAINSONG AND THE CONTRAPUNTAL PERIOD

Adler, Guido, *Handbuch der Musikgeschichte*, vol. I (2d ed.; Berlin: H. Keller, 1930)

Ambros, A. W., and Leichtentritt, Hugo, *Geschichte der Musik*, vol. IV (2d ed.; Leipzig: F. E. C. Leuckart, 1909)

Arnold, J. H., *Plainsong Accompaniment* (London: Oxford University Press, 1927)

Burney, Charles, *A General History of Music*, vol. II (new ed.; New York: Harcourt, Brace and Co., 1935)

Haydon, Glen, *The Evolution of the Six-Four Chord* (Berkeley: University of California Press, 1933)

Indy, d', Vincent, *Cours de composition musicale*, vol. I (5th ed; Paris: Durand et fils, 1912)

Jeppesen, Knud, *Kontrapunkt* (Leipzig: Breitkopf and Härtel, 1935)

——, *Counterpoint* (New York: Prentice-Hall, 1939), translated by Glen Haydon

——, *The Style of Palestrina and the Dissonance* (London: Oxford University Press, 1927)

Leichtentritt, Hugo, *Geschichte der Motette* (Leipzig: Breitkopf and Härtel, 1908)

Martini, F. G., *Saggio fondamentale pratico di contrapunto*, 2 vols. (Bologna, 1774)

Morris, R. O., *Contrapuntal Technique in the Sixteenth Century* (Oxford: The Clarendon Press, 1922)

Prunières, Henry, *Nouvelle Histoire de la musique*, vol. I (Paris: Editions Rieder, 1934)

Rockstro, W. S., "Ecclesiastical Modes," *Grove's Dictionary of Music and Musicians*, vol. III (3rd ed.; New York: The Macmillan Co., 1927)

Wooldridge, H. E., *The Oxford History of Music*, vol. II (2d ed.; London: Oxford University Press, 1932)

——, "Studies in the Technique of Sixteenth-Century Music," *Musical Antiquary*, January 1912–April 1913

II. COLLECTIONS OF CONTRAPUNTAL MUSIC BY IMPORTANT COMPOSERS OF THE FIFTEENTH, SIXTEENTH, AND SEVENTEENTH CENTURIES

Ambros, A. W., *Geschichte der Musik*, vol. v (3rd ed.; Leipzig: Breitkopf and Härtel, 1911)

Attaingnant, Pierre, *Treize Livres de motets*, ed. A. Smijers, 3 vols. (Paris: Lyre Bird Press, 1934–38)

Byrd, William, *Collected Vocal Works*, 9 vols., ed E. H. Fellowes (London: Stainer and Bell, 1937–39)

——, *Tudor Church Music*, vols. ii, vii, ix (London: Oxford University Press, 1922, 1927, 1928)

Chorwerk, Das, ed. Friederich Blume, 9 vols. (Wolfenbüttel: Kallmeyer, 1929–38)

Commer, Franz, *Musica Sacra*, 28 vols. (Berlin: Bote and Bock, 1839–87)

Denkmäler deutscher Tonkunst (Leipzig: Breitkopf and Härtel, 1892–1937)

Denkmäler der Tonkunst in Bayern (Leipzig: Breitkopf and Härtel, 1894–1937)

Denkmäler der Tonkunst in Österreich (Vienna: Artaria, 1894–1937)

Des Prés, Josquin, *Werken*, ed. A. Smijers, 17 vols. (Leipzig: Kistner and Siegel, 1925–37)

English Madrigal School, 36 vols. (London: Stainer and Bell, 1913–24)

Hispaniae Schola musica sacra, ed. Felipe Pedrell, 8 vols. (Barcelona: Pujol, 1894–98)

Istituzione e monumenti dell' arte musicale, 5 vols. (Milan: Ricordi, 1931–34)

Lasso, Orlando di, *Magnum opus musicum*, odd-numbered vols. of the *Sämmtliche Werke* (Leipzig: Breitkopf and Härtel, 1894–1926)

——, *Septem Psalmi Poenitentiales*, ed. Hermann Bäuerle (Leipzig: Breitkopf and Härtel, 1905)

Les Maîtres Musiciens de la Renaissance française, ed. Henri Expert, 23 vols. (Paris: Senart, 1894–1908)

Monte, Philippi de, *Opera*, 26 vols. (Düsseldorf: Schwann, 1930?–35)

Monteverdi, Claudio, *Tutte le opere*, ed. G. Francesco Malipiero, 14 vols. (Asolo, 1926–32)

Obrecht, Jakob, *Werken*, ed. Johannes Wolf, 30 vols. (Leipzig: Breitkopf and Härtel, 1912–21)

Ockeghem, Johannes, *Sämtliche Werke*, in *Publikationen Älterer Musik* (Leipzig: Breitkopf and Härtel, 1927–)

Palestrina, da, Giovanni Pierluigi, *Opera omnia* (Leipzig: Breitkopf and Härtel, 1862–1903)

Proske, Karl, *Musica Divina*, 2 vols., 5 secs. (Regensburg, 1853–55)

Purcell, Henry, *Works*, 26 vols. (London: Novello and Co., Ltd. 1878–1928)

Riemann, Hugo, *Musikgeschichte in Beispielen* (4th ed.; Leipzig: Breitkopf and Härtel, 1929)

Rochlitz, Friedrich, *Sammlung vorzüglicher Gesangstücke*, 3 vols. (Mainz: B. Schotts Söhnen, 1838–40)

Schering, Arnold, *Geschichte der Musik in Beispielen* (Leipzig: Breitkopf and Härtel, 1931)

Schütz, Heinrich, *Sämmtliche Werke*, ed. Philipp Spitta, 16 vols. and supplement (Leipzig: Breitkopf and Härtel, 1885–94)

Tallis, Thomas, in *Tudor Church Music*, vol. vi (London: Oxford University Press, 1928)

Torchi, Luigi, *L'Arte musicale in Italia*, vols. i, ii (Milan: Ricordi, 1897)

Tudor Church Music, 10 vols. (London: Oxford University Press, 1923–29), octavo ed., nos. 1–68

Victoria, T. L., *Opera omnia*, ed. Felipe Pedrell, 8 vols. (Leipzig: Breitkopf and Härtel, 1902–13)